R BK   792.028   F492A
AUDITION. A COMPLETE GUIDE FOR ACTORS WITH AN
     ANNOTATED SELECTION OF   /FINCH
     C1984   16.95   FV

W9-DEA-139

3000 675920 30013
St. Louis Community College

792.028 F492a   FV
FINCHLEY
AUDITION! A COMPLETE GUIDE
FOR ACTORS WITH AN ANNOTATED
SELECTION OF READINGS   16.95

WITHDRAWN

St. Louis Community College

Library

5801 Wilson Avenue
St. Louis, Missouri 63110

Joan Finchley, a professional actress and dramatic teacher, has taught acting at Boston University, New York University, and the Western Australian Academy of Performing Arts.

AUDITION!

A Complete Guide for Actors with an Annotated Selection of Readings

JOAN FINCHLEY

A SPECTRUM BOOK

Prentice-Hall, Inc., Englewood Cliffs, New Jersey 07632

Library of Congress Cataloging in Publication Data

Finchley, Joan.
    Audition! : a complete guide for actors with an
annotated selection of readings.

    "A Spectrum Book."
    Includes index.
    1. Monologues.   2. Acting—Auditions.   I. Title.
PN2080.F56   1984   792'.028   84-9943
ISBN 0-13-052093-4
ISBN 0-13-052085-3 (pbk.)

© 1984 by Prentice-Hall, Inc., Englewood Cliffs, New Jersey 07632.
All rights reserved. No part of this book may be reproduced in any form
or by any means without permission in writing from the publisher.
A Spectrum Book. Printed in the United States of America.

10 9 8 7 6 5 4 3 2 1

This book is available at a special discount when ordered
in bulk quantities. Contact Prentice-Hall, Inc., General
Publishing Division, Special Sales, Englewood Cliffs, N.J. 07632.

Editorial/production supervision by Chris McMorrow
Cover design by Hal Siegel

ISBN 0-13-052093-4

ISBN 0-13-052085-3 {PBK.}

PRENTICE-HALL INTERNATIONAL, INC., *London*
PRENTICE-HALL OF AUSTRALIA PTY. LIMITED, *Sydney*
PRENTICE-HALL CANADA INC., *Toronto*
PRENTICE-HALL OF INDIA PRIVATE LIMITED, *New Delhi*
PRENTICE-HALL OF JAPAN, INC., *Tokyo*
PRENTICE-HALL OF SOUTHEAST ASIA PTE. LTD., *Singapore*
WHITEHALL BOOKS LIMITED, *Wellington, New Zealand*
EDITORA PRENTICE-HALL DO BRASIL LTDA., *Rio de Janeiro*

FOR NAÏLA AND FOR DALE

———————————————————————————

CONTENTS

FOREWORD

The Actor's Needs

The need of a young actor to act is stronger than the intelligent layman can understand. The world might think that this ambition is motivated by the desire for money, success, and fame. Even if the actor says this is his aim, it is still only partially true. If there could be a slogan, it would be: "Join the theatre and give back to the world part of the greatness each young actor feels is in him." The actor is fighting for a way of life. The theatre differs from many other professions because it is a way of life.

Acting as an expression includes a rare thing—soul satisfaction—which is not very concrete, yet very important to his growth. If you don't understand that acting has this level of expression, that it is an art form, you are only adding to the confusion which already exists.

The material presented here includes many, many ways in which the actor might present himself to those who need to see him work on his craft.

The unusually varied selections will open many interesting doors, both for the actor and his audience.

Along with other creative powers released in the actor,

Miss Finchley's book will challenge him as he grows to the whole range of dramatic literature.

Everyday reality is not enough for the actor. He must find an art form with which to express this reality—life! When he becomes an actor, he achieves an independence and an ability to grow as long as he lives. Even if you take the platform away from him, he will grow; he has the tools, the training, and the discipline. To grow is his deepest and truest need when he says: "I want to be an actor."

STELLA ADLER

PREFACE

Auditioning is an unnatural act. I can think of few professions in which a prospective employee, applying for a job, must present himself or herself in the manner that actors do. Can you imagine an automobile mechanic walking into a garage and being told he must reassemble an engine in front of, say, 30 other mechanics before getting the job? Or imagine a pastry chef being asked to bake strudel in front of 30 Hungarian restaurant owners! That would be *one crowded kitchen!*

Besides being unnatural, auditioning is an act whose rewards are uncertain. As we in the professional theatre all know, the casting of a show has often already been done over rounds of beer and cups of coffee. If anyone complains, the director can always say, "Sorry, ducks, but I didn't like your audition." In amateur productions, roles are often assigned to the actor or actress who can also help with the lighting when Ralph gets ill.

Unnatural? For certain. Inequitable? Surely that. Solutions? None at the moment. The system is here to stay.

Two positive ways of confronting the situation are (1) to experiment with the audition guidelines set forth in this book, and (2) to discover and develop fresh, first-rate literature with which to audition.

My primary intention in writing this book is to aid in the selection of that literature. The book contains nondramatic audition material (fiction, nonfiction, poetry, and newspaper and magazine articles) for the professional theatre artist and for the student of drama.

Unconventional material can be of extraordinary value to an actor because a casting director or teacher has fewer assumptions and expectations about the piece. The circumstances and biography of a character's life can be created from your own imagination and tailored to your own needs. You are not at the mercy of both the character and the play's reputation.

For example, in *A Streetcar Named Desire*, Blanche DuBois is an elegant, delicate, and sensual lady from the South who later escapes into a psychotic world when things go wrong. Allan Felix in *Play It Again, Sam* is homely, nervous, and shy and has difficulty meeting women.

To illustrate further: Over the course of a casting day, a director is likely to hear 15 versions of Blanche DuBois or Allan Felix. Rather than concentrate on your acting skills, the director is unhappily comparing your performance with the one(s) he or she so fondly recalls: namely Vivien Leigh's or Uta Hagen's. (Of course, as you move farther away from Broadway, associations such as these become less frequent.) With the Allan Felix role, none of the 15 versions the director has just witnessed will ever compare with his own brillant performance of that role in a recent dinner theatre engagement in Paramus, New Jersey.

The same values can apply to directors. By being receptive to nondramatic audition material, your mind is freed from past associations with the selection you are hearing. You are able to concentrate *solely* on the actor's performance. A director once told me she welcomed unconventional material because it helped her gain further insight into the actor "as a person." An actor's choices can often reflect his or her personality.

This book is not an indictment of conventional plays; I fully acknowledge their value as timely works of art. However, parting with certain musty classics, at least for audition purposes, could prove to be a wise choice. Nondramatic selections contain all the essential elements of a good audition piece: rich language, vivid images, and an expansive emotional range.

On page 2 the excerpt from *Voice and the Actor* by Cicely Berry—copyright 1973 by Cicely Berry—is reprinted by permission of MacMillan Publishing Company and Harrap Ltd.

A selection from *Even Cowgirls Get the Blues* by Tom Robbins, copyright © 1976 by Thomas Robbins, is reprinted by permission of Bantam Books, Inc. All rights reserved.

Selections from *Working: People Talk About What They Do All Day and How They Feel About What They Do* by Studs Terkel are reprinted with permission of Random House, Inc. and the author.

The excerpt from *Getting Even*, by Woody Allen is reprinted by permission of Random House, Inc. and the author.

Portions of *Sophie's Choice* by William Styron are used with the permission of Random House, Inc. and the author.

The selection from Studs Terkel's *American Dreams: Lost and Found*, copyright 1980 by Studs Terkel, published by Pantheon Books, a Division of Random House, Inc., is used by permission.

"Letter II" from *Mark Twain's Letters from the Earth*, edited by Bernard DeVoto, copyright ©1962 by the Mark Twain Co., is reprinted by permission of Harper & Row, Publishers, Inc.

The selection from *The Village Voice*, "Baby Gets a Tattoo," copyright © 1981 Deanne Stillman is used by permission of the author.

Excerpts from Kathy Kahn's *Hillbilly Woman* copyright © 1973 by Kathy Kahn are reprinted by permission of Doubleday & Company, Inc.

Excerpts from Morton Dauwen Zabel's *The Art of Ruth Draper: Her Dramas and Characters*, copyright © 1960 by Morton Dauwen Zabel, are reprinted by permission of Doubleday & Company, Inc., and Sylvia Dauwen and Margerite Dauwen.

The excerpt from Phyllis Theroux's *California and Other States of Grace*, William Morrow and Company, Inc., 1980, is used by permission of the publisher.

The excerpts from "Diary of a Rent Striker" appearing in the New York Herald Tribune, 1964, © I.H.T. Corporation, are reprinted by permission.

Material on pages 74–77 is from *Children in Jail*, copyright ©
1977 by Thomas J. Cottle.

Pages 78–79 contain an excerpt from *Raging Bull* by Jake La
Motta with Hoseph Carter and Peter Savage. Copyright © 1970 by
Jake La Motta. Reprinted by permission of Bantam Books, Inc. All rights
reserved.

The excerpts from the *1973 Rape Investigations Report* are used
by permission of the Memphis Police Department.

The excerpt from Faith McNulty's *The Burning Bed*, published
by Harcourt Brace Janovich, 1980, is used by permission.

Material from *Nam: The Vietman War in the Words of the
Men and Women Who Fought There* by Mark Baker is used by permission of William Morrow & Company, Inc.

Material from *Dispatches* by Michael Herr and *First Person
America* by Ann Banks is used by permission of Random House, Inc.

The selections "Plymouth Rock Joe" and "Elizabeth Childers"
from Edgar Lee Master's *Spoon River Anthology*, published by MacMillan Publishing Co., Inc., are used by permission of Ellen C. Masters.

The selection taken from *Growing Up Southern*, edited by
Chris Mayfield, © 1981 Pantheon Books, A Division of Random
House, Inc., is used by permission.

The poems taken from The *Common Muse: An Anthology of
Popular British Ballads and Poetry* (XV-XXth Centuries), edited by V.
de Sola Pinto and A. E. Rodway, 1957, are quoted by permission of
the Philosophical Library, Inc.

The two poems by Emily Dickinson, "I Felt a Funeral in My Brain"
and "I Like to See It Lap the Miles" are reprinted by permission of the
publishers and the Trustees of Amherst College from THE POEMS OF
EMILY DICKINSON, edited by Thomas H. Johnson, Cambridge,
Mass.: The Belknap Press of Harvard University Press, Copyright 1951,
©1955, 1979 by the President and Fellows of Harvard College.

HOW TO USE
THIS BOOK

1

Several selections in this book appear in their entirety. Because of stringent copyright laws, however, I have excerpted many, giving the reader only impressions of their language and content. Where permission to reproduce a piece (in any form) has been denied, I have chosen to describe it instead.

The selections are briefly summarized. These summaries are not intended as literary criticism but, rather, are designed to highlight facts and assumptions about the character and circumstances.

The nature of this book disallows categorizing the selections by age or gender. Instead, I have grouped them by subject matter and style. The first 18 selections are mainly humorous and contemporary character studies: "Popping Up in 60 Minutes," Erma Bombeck, Woody Allen. The next 16 selections are sociological/psychological character studies: *Children in Jail, In Cold Blood.* The seven selections that follow deal mainly in Americana: *Hillbilly Women, Growing Up Southern.*

The final section is devoted entirely to poetry. Rarely is an actor called upon to audition with (nondramatic) poetic material. However, poetry does have a strong place and purpose in training the young actor who is preparing for classical roles. It can be an excellent springboard in mastering the works of Shakespeare, Webster, Congreve, and the like. Poetry provides the imagery, rhythm, meter, figurative language, and musical devices that must be comprehended if an actor wishes to perform classical, dramatic works.

In *Voice and the Actor* Cicely Berry comments on the value of poetry in training the actor's voice:

> . . . the demands it makes are very particular and quite subtle, yet its extravagance encourages you to do extravagant things which are not untrue. This has nothing to do with what kind of acting you want to do; it is not just for the person who wants to do mainly classical acting but for those using all kinds of text. The point is, you find inflections happen which, if they had been calculated, would seem false but which, if they spring from the stimulation of a text, are quite true. Speeches from plays are not always helpful as they cannot be done without

reference to character and interpretation and other issues than voice immediately become important.

Out of the vast repertoire of British and American poetry, selecting which poems to use was no easy task. Many of them were chosen because they illustrate well the aforementioned literary elements—imagery, meter, rhythm, and so on—whereas others seem to embody more dramatic elements: character, action, and different levels of emotion. In the end, I asked my own students which ones were both useful and pleasurable to them.

Before each selection, you will find the title of the source. If it suits your needs, obtain the source (readily available at good libraries and bookstores), which, of course, contains the material in its entirety. To further assist you, I have included the author, publisher, date of publication, specific page(s) where the piece begins and ends, and an indication of whether the specific pages are from the paperback or hardcover edition. Although I have suggested age and gender, no overall rule applies. Much of this material can be performed by a range of ages and by actors of either sex.

Next, you will find an abbreviation of the type of audition circumstance the material is best suited for (see chart below). A scene from *Sophie's Choice* would not be recommended for the Turnpike Dinner Theatre, nor would "Popping Up in 60 Minutes" be apropos for a classical repertory company.

Repertory Theatre	REP
Off-Broadway	OB
Summer Stock	SS
Dinner Theatre	DT
Drama School/	
Acting Class	DS
Agents	A

Finally, after each piece there is a section entitled "Treatment." I offer brief insights into the character, content, or style of the piece and at times suggest a few acting guidelines to help you get started. This section is not meant to be an intensive character study nor a lengthy acting manual. My hope is simply to provide the actor with a base from which to work.

To avoid redundancy, I often refer you to characters from other selections because the emotional levels, content, and style are similar. The same guidelines can be considered for other characters.

This format is slightly altered in the poetry section. All the poems appear in their entirety, and only where the selection is obscure do I note its source. The audition circumstance is left to the actor's own discretion. Realistically, however, the best place for the performance of these poems would probably be the classroom.

Unlike dramatic literature, poetry is not always clearly defined with regard to character, intent, or circumstance, and for the most part is a personal experience. With that considered, I have resisted the temptation to include summaries and/or acting guidelines as I do with the other nondramatic selections in this book. For the insatiable scholar, an oversupply of literary criticism is readily available in every library and/or college bookstore.

The greatest effort on the part of actor, director, or teacher lies in the editing. All of these selections need to be neatly trimmed down to a realistic playing time, usually 3–5 minutes. Editing material for audition purposes is a highly subjective process. What appeals to one actor may seem insignificant and mundane to another. The best method of editing is to ask yourself these questions:

1. What fascinates me about what the character says?
2. What part(s) of the speech do I personally connect with?
3. Which parts of the speech provide the best dramatic possibilities?
4. Which parts best reveal information about the character's intentions and feelings?

The rest is oftentimes excess, and you can easily eliminate it without obstructing the clarity or content of the speech.

If you have the luxury of time, you will want to read the entire text of the source as you would any dramatic script. The process of investigating this material can be stimulating and informative and can hopefully lead you down other paths. It serves a twofold purpose: the discovery of first-rate audition material and exposure to a diverse body of literature.

All the material in this book has been "tested" by actors, writers, directors, and teachers. It was through their cumulative opinions that the final selections were made.

FOOD
FOR THOUGHT

2

A good chef would agree that haute cuisine cannot be created without adhering to the advice and instructions given in a first-rate cookbook. Similar rules apply to the audition process. There is a basic recipe that the actor must tend to. Once you have learned the recipe, cook the meal. If the meal turns out well, is tasty and esthetically pleasing, you have done your job. Relax and enjoy your creation. If the meal turns out poorly and your taste buds tell you it is far from a culinary delight, a few options are available to remedy the situation:

> Repeat the recipe
> Change the recipe
> Discard the recipe

Such is the case with the audition guidelines that appear in the following section. It is important to remember that no two actors are alike. What fills the need (and gets the job) for one actor may be unsuitable for you. Always remain flexible. A rigid actor is a dead one.

At the end of this section, I refer you to a few good books on acting and auditioning to further assist your mission. But proceed with caution: you cannot learn about acting from any text. You can be guided, but you cannot be taught.

While writing this book, I met a well-known actress who won an Academy Award for her performance in a recent film. She told me: "I hate books about acting; I've never read one. I got to where I am today by just *doing* it. By throwing myself into the ring—again and again and again and then once more."

For this reason, I have resisted all temptation to turn the following chapter into a didactic treatise. Instead, I have chosen those guidelines which are commonly overlooked by most actors, both professional *and* amateur.

Further Reading

Respect for Acting by Uta Hagen with Haskel Frankel. New York: Macmillan, Inc., 1973.

Audition by Michael Shurtleff.
New York: Walker Publishing Company, 1978.

Presence of the Actor by Joseph Chaiken.
New York: Atheneum Publishers, 1980.

THE RECIPE

3

Keep a File

My undergraduate days were spent at a first-rate theatre training school. One semester, since the school was in close proximity to New York City, I applied for permission to pursue an independent study on audition techniques (anything to get out of Beginning Lighting Design 101).

I was well aware I could not accept an acting job (should I have actually landed one), because my primary commitment was to the training program. But I welcomed the restriction. It freed me from the tension and despair ("Please, God, I need this job!") that seemed to be the plight of so many actors I observed. I knew my day would come soon enough. Instead, I went from "mock audition" to "mock audition" watching, waiting, participating. I kept a note card on each audition I attended and ended up with a file much in the form of a diary, which I still refer to now and then. Sometimes when I look at it, I swallow hard and say, "I can't believe I used to do that." Here are a few entries from it:

> Attended an audition for a musical comedy today. Chose to sing a tune from a musical currently running on Broadway. Knew it was the wrong choice when I heard a loud "ugh" coming from the dark. The auditors were tired of it. My guess is they had heard that song at least fifty times that day.

Moral: Do not choose a song from a current show. Wait until its reputation has a chance to simmer.

> This week I met with a well-known acting teacher, to audition for a place in his acting class. We chatted extensively. I wondered at what point he was going to ask the inevitable question: "What are you going to do for me?" He never did. Instead he simply said, "You're very good, aren't you?" I looked him straight in the eye, and with all the conviction I could muster up replied, "Yes, I am."

Moral: If given the opportunity to converse with an auditor, take full advantage. Demonstrate your sincerity, wit, charm, and intelligence. Remain positive about yourself and your talent. (P.S. I never had to do my audition piece, and was invited to join the class.)

If you are inexperienced at the audition game, I recommend travelling this route. For the well-seasoned actor, I am not encouraging auditioning for the sake of auditioning, but I do wish to convey the importance of simply keeping a record. This system is as valuable as any "How to Audition" class might be and surely more economical.

Being Seen

Regardless of how wonderful a performance you give, it will not matter if it cannot be seen. If you are auditioning in a legitimate theatre equipped with at least a few lighting instruments, take a moment to find the light. That is where your audition should take place, not in the dark. If uncertain as to whether you are in the light, simply ask the auditors. They will be more than happy to tell you.

In many instances, you will find yourself auditioning in well-lit rehearsal studios, hotel rooms, or classrooms. Chances are you will have no control over the situation and will not have to concern yourself with the lighting.

Being Heard

If given the opportunity, find out *beforehand* in what size room your audition will take place. Then, adjust your vocal range accordingly. Many actors misinterpret the term projecting to mean shouting. If you do not know the size of the audition space, be prepared to shift vocal gears at a moment's notice.

The best preparation is to rehearse your scene in different-sized rooms. Ask a friend to sit in the last row and note which sections of your speech are inaudible or incomprehensible. Sharpening this skill involves extensive vocal training. For your assistance I refer you to *Voice and the Actor* by Cicely Berry (Macmillan Publishing Company, Inc., 1973) and *Freeing the Natural Voice* by Kristen Linklater (Drama Book Specialists, 1976). Both, however, will be of more value under the tutelage of a proper vocal coach.

Attire

If attending a general audition, go for the unobtrusive look. Garish outfits can impede an auditor's ability to concentrate on your audition. But if you are being considered for a specific role, dress appropriately. For example, if the role is Masha from *The Three Sisters*, you might best save your designer jeans for another occasion.

Warming Up

The purpose of warming up before an audition is to tune and relax the actor's instrument. Every actor knows what works for him or her. Some vocalize, others meditate, still others run their speech 50 times backwards. If you need to work this way and insist on warming up a few minutes before the actual audition, by all means proceed. The best place to prepare is *at home*. Quiet, private spaces are rarely available at the audition site. For me, the ladies' room never quite fits the bill.

Do what *you* have to do. However, keep in mind that it is unrealistic to think you can achieve a proper vocal, physical and psychological warm-up under adverse conditions. I would aim for one of the above. Many actors I know prefer an activity that has little to do with the audition itself: reading, balancing your checkbook, or writing letters.

Most professional actors will tell you that when acting becomes a full-time career and auditioning a way of life, the need for extensive preparation of this nature will subside. You just go do it!

Get Help

You can rehearse a scene or monologue numerous times. Hopefully you will improve upon it with each run-through, but you can reach a point where monitoring yourself becomes impossible. Find an audience. It does not necessarily have to be an acting teacher. Try the speech on anyone who will listen to you: friends, parents, landlords, exterminators. By rehearsing for a diverse audience, you will gain the confidence so needed when the time comes to perform. This process will will answer an all-important question: "Do I know it?"

I think the ultimate test of confidence is to run into a shoe store, find the nearest clerk, and begin reciting your piece. If he doesn't call the cops—that is, if he *believes* you—then you're a success!

Eye Contact

You have several options available:

1. You can address imaginary characters in empty chairs (place them downstage, please), but it is unnecessary to focus the entire speech on them. The auditors accept the convention; they know the characters are part of your scene. *Refer* to the characters from time to time, but do not remain immobilized in front of them. In real life, no one stares directly into the eyes of a person they are talking to, for the entire time.

2. If auditioning for *one* auditor, some actors like to make direct eye contact. If relieves them of the burden of talking to make-believe people. But be careful. Some auditors are threatened and uncomfortable with direct confrontation. Others may

welcome the intimacy of it. So ask. Simply say; "Do you mind if I use you?"

3. If you are auditioning for several auditors and your speech is of the "Friends, Romans, countrymen" genre, address the entire group, and no one auditor will feel uneasy. This technique can heighten the effect of your speech and presence on the stage.

Props

True, props can be your friend. They are an additional tool in the acting process, since they reveal information about your character and can further the action of a scene. However, the very nature of the audition situation is one of anxiety and stress. One less thing to worry about is one less thing that can go wrong. Every actor has his or her story to tell about the lighter that wouldn't light or the alarm clock that refused to go off. For some mysterious reason, the gods are never on our side when we need them. *Minimize your props.*

Dialects

Unless requested to do so, avoid dialects. Actors often mistake the use of dialects for good acting. They get caught up in the rhythmic flow of the dialect and forget the scene's real intentions. If you must use one, rehearse the scene in your own speech, tagging the dialect on last. If you have a sharp ear for language, recordings are the best source for learning dialects.

Further reading

Foreign Dialects: A Manual for Actors, Directors and Writers, by Lewis Herman and Marguerite Shalett Herman. New York: Theatre Arts Books, 1973.

More Stage Dialects by Jerry Blunt.
New York: Harper & Row, 1980.

A Pronouncing Dictionary of American English by John S.
Kenyon and Thomas A. Knott. Springfield, MA: G. & C. Merriam Company, 1953.

Choice of Material

Choose something you like. If you rehearse your piece a few times and discover it isn't working, drop it. If you do not, the piece can become your nemesis, making the work sheer drudgery.

Choose a piece whose speaker is close to your age and suitable to your physical attributes. If you do not know yourself well enough, seek the advice of someone you trust. Your choice should say something about you, reflecting your personality, intelligence, and imagination.

Just in case you are asked to do something else, do not be caught off guard. Always have extra material *prepared.* I recommend knowing five classical and five contemporary speeches, ready to be performed at a moment's notice. To best demonstrate your versatility and range, these selections should be of a contrasting nature.

Being prepared in this manner shows the auditors you are a serious actor who has done his or her homework and knows what the audition game is all about.

Obtain the Script

If you know what role you are auditioning for, obtain a copy of the script beforehand. Take full advantage of the opportunity by reading it thoroughly and becoming very familiar with your particular scene(s).

Your responsibility does not end there. Familiarity with a text does not mean you can act it. Make some decisions about the scene. What does my character want? What is my relationship to the other characters in the scene? One can *never* know what a director wants, and it is usually a waste of precious time to try to find out. By making specific choices, you have something to go on, something to play.

Listen to yourself and enjoy what you have prepared. I know an actor (employed and successful) who, before each audition, gives this little speech: "If I am on the wrong track and interpreting the script contrary to your vision, please stop me." It saves their time and yours. If you are doing good work, chances are they will not stop you.

Cold Readings

If you ask, most directors will allow you to have a look at the script before your reading. But *you* have to ask. If the reply is negative, don't fret. You will never know what you are capable of doing unless you try. This could be your chance to shine. With spontaneity, humor, and great aplomb, accept the challenge. Travel this unknown territory as if you have been there a thousand times!

Résumés

A few simple rules here, and you are in business. Produce an 8 × 10 black and white photograph with a résumé attached. Both items must represent you accurately: a picture that looks like you and a résumé that is truthful.

While I was teaching at a well-known university one summer, my students were constantly asking, "What if my credits are few and far between?" My reply was simply, "So what?" List them anyway and never apologize. Bow down to no one. Do not confuse subservience with modesty: the former is obsequious, the latter essential.

Waiting Room Etiquette and Survival

An open audition is one that everyone and anyone may attend—and does. Waiting long hours at audition centers, surrounded by other contenders, may be unnecessary for you at the career stage you have arrived at. Presumably you have something called a scheduled appointment. If so, count your blessings and feel free to skip this section.

I handed these questions to a group of actors I interviewed at an open audition call in New York City. The actors I spoke to are named Kenn, Jacki, Janis, and Donna.

What happens when you sign up to audition early in the day and realize you won't be called on for several hours? What do you do with your time?

KENN: I use the time well. I make sure I have a list—made the night before—of constructive activities I can accomplish. I catch up on letter writing, read, make phone calls.

JACKI: I'm the queen of the coffee shops. I patronize one after the other. One more Danish and I'll be ready for Weight Watchers!

JANIS: I go home. Now and then I check in to see how fast things are moving.

What if you don't live near the audition site?

JANIS: I have friends all over this town. If I know I'm going to be near one of them, I'll drop by. At least it's a quiet place to rest. I phone the night before. If they're not going to be home, I manage to get a set of keys. Why, I've got keys to over a dozen apartments in this city.

What makes "hanging around" the audition site so objectionable?

KENN: Are you kidding? It scatters your energy and deflates your morale.

How so?

KENN: Some actors can be disrespectful and unrestrained. You get sucked into their conversations. It's impossible not to eavesdrop.

Usually conversations about the negative aspects of the business—the job they didn't get, the director who was a tyrant, or the show that closed. It's okay to complain, I'm not saying that. But do they have to do it for all the world to hear?

DONNA: It really kills me when they start showing their latest photos and résumés. I don't think the audition waiting room is the place for it. I guess I'm just uptight about competition and don't need to be reminded of what I'm up against. I'm nervous enough thinking about my audition.

KENN: Acting/auditioning is about talking yourself *into it*. By participating in or encouraging negative patter, you defeat that frame of mind.

Isn't there a quiet place you can escape to?

DONNA: If there is, I'm usually the first one to find it!

Beware the Beast

By the tender age of nine, I had relinquished all belief in mythical creatures. Santa Claus, the tooth fairy, the stork and the boogieman would have to find housing elsewhere, for I was on to bigger and better things.

When I entered the acting profession, it was frightening to learn that one of these creatures had resurfaced. Namely, the boogieman. He was back. He returned in the form of a fat, cigar-smoking "gentleman," promising fame, fortune, and the opportunity of a lifetime. There is usually a price for the promises he will make and never keep. Don't pay it! Keep your clothes on and slam the door loudly as you exit.

You may be asking, "How will I know if I am doing business with a shady non-professional?" A few clues: he likes to disguise himself as an agent, producer, casting director, mentor, or acting teacher. He can usually be found holding auditions at his apartment (instead of a bona fide audition center), casting an all-nude version of *Uncle Vanya,* or crediting himself for the successful careers of well-known celebrities ("I gave Julie Harris her first lucky break").

Chances are you will fall prey to such a beast at least once in your career—chalk it up to experience and take heed next time.

Every actor has his or her story to tell. An actress described the following experience:

It had been a slow year with few acting jobs in sight. I was getting bored and restless. In response to an ad in the trade papers, I sent a photo and résumé to a casting director in Caracas, Venezuela. They were looking for a young actress to play the lead role in a feature film. Several months later I received a telegram:

Dear Ms. Smith,

After considering hundreds of actors, we have cast you in our film. We will be contacting you in the very near future to discuss your availability.

A transatlantic telephone call soon followed the telegram. An appointment was made for the next week. I was to meet the producer and director at a hotel in New York City to obtain a script and sign the necessary contracts ($2500 a week!!). I hung the phone up and screamed for ten minutes: "There is a God! I've gotten a job!" My bags were packed.

When I arrived at the hotel I was met by a little man who barely spoke English. (Where were the producers and director?) He wanted me to "read" for him. Since this was the first mention of an audition, it certainly made sense to do so. He pushed a button on a cassette recorder. Wild jungle music came blasting out of the tiny machine. I thought Johnny Weismuller would come swinging by any minute.

My suspicions were already beginning, but I decided not to prejudge the situation. I *desperately* wanted this to be real. I *needed* this to be real. A bit later, the little man narrated from the script and asked me to "act out" the following directions:

As you run frantically through the jungle you stumble and fall to the ground. Upon looking up, a young woman appears, claiming to be a Lesbian Countess. You are immediately seduced by her beauty and kindness. You take The Countess in your arms (jungle music building) and kiss her passionately. Clumsily, you begin to remove your clothing. . .

Need I go on? I walked over to the cassette player and clicked it off. I asked the gentleman one question: "What is the name of this film?" He replied, "Barbara, The Lesbian Countess of Caracas." (A Venezuelan named Barbara??) I knew I had been had. I gathered my things and headed for the door. (He pleaded with me to stay, apologizing profusely.) As I approached the elevator in the lobby I saw a young woman get off. I could tell by her appearance that she was the next victim. I cornered the woman and relayed my experience, strongly advising her not to go in. When I finished my diatribe she looked at me and said, "I'm going in anyway—just in case."

If You Blow It

If you forget your lines or feel you have gotten off to a bad start, ask if you may begin again. The answer will usually be yes. The best advice is not to lose control and end up hating yourself when it is over. With each audition, it gets easier and easier. Really it does.

Occasionally, there is a bright side to our blunders, as illustrated in this good letter I received from a young actress:

Dear Joan,

I was recently reminded of an incident I witnessed a few years back.

I was at The Southeastern Theatre Conference (S.E.T.C.) spring auditions where hundreds of actors, singers, and fire jugglers are herded through a crowded assembly hall with one minute and eight bars of music to prove their worth. I was number 317.

Number 316 was ushered to the stage. He nodded to the accompanist to push the button on the portable cassette player he had brought with him. "We got sunlight on the sand. . ." He went stone blank. The tinny recording played on enthusiastically. A sympathetic producer (really!) sang softly to the frozen, white-faced young man, to try and get him back on the track: "We got mangoes and bananas you can pick right off the tree. . ." The producers at nearby tables joined in: "We got volleyball and ping pong and a lot of dandy games. . ." The young man began to nod vaguely: "What ain't we got?" Everyone, at the top of their lungs—"We ain't got dames!"

The room exploded in thunderous applause and cheers!! The young man, having finally been awakened from his stupor, bowed and exited. Unfortunately for me, the laughing and cheering hadn't subsided when my minute and eight bars began. But I gave it my shot. A couple of hours later, I took a look at the callback board. Do you know that creep 316 got called back by everybody there?

Truly,
Miriam D.

Eavesdropping: Snippets of Conversation Overheard at Audition Calls

"Auditioning has nothing to do with acting. Once you get the job, a new set of rules applies. Your responsibilities are to the work. You no longer have to sell yourself; you've already done that. You've been bought."

"The theatre is a wonderful life if you are fortunate enough to be working in it."

"The theatre is a terrible life. I should have gone to medical school."

"I just keep in mind that auditioning is part of being an actor. This is my job. Some folks punch a clock—I wake up every morning, I audition. I'm just not getting paid, that's all."

"Why am I here? Well . . . when I wake up in the morning, I just can't think of anything I'd rather do with my life."

"I'm doing everything I can do. I sent photos and résumés, I audition for everything and anything, I talk with agents, I talk with directors, I talk to my psychiatrist. It may seem like a waste of time—it is to my parents. But at least when I'm old and gray, I can say I tried, I did everything I could."

"I like to pretend that the two-minute auditions I give three days a week *are* my performances. My audition *is* the show. It opens and closes in two minutes, the same day. But that's okay because I'm grateful there's another two-minute show to do tomorrow. It's when the auditions stop—when there just isn't anything to go to—that's when I'll panic. That's when I'd better stop dreaming."

"Auditioning gives me a chance to memorize some wonderful works of literature. It's a great feeling to know I can recite practically anything from Shakespeare to Sam Shepard at the drop of a hat."

"I met my wife at an audition."

"The way I see it, with unemployment soaring in every other profession, why not be an actor? I would feel really envious if all my non-actor friends were gainfully employed in their chosen fields. But they're not. Be an actor, the time is ripe!

When It's Over

When you have finished the audition, go home. Forget about it. Once you leave, there is nothing more you can do. Fill your life with activities which have little to do with acting and the business of acting. Go to karate class, write your memoirs, cook a great dinner. Promise you will not sit home and wait for the phone to ring!

A little voice in me is saying, "Great advice to give, impossible to take." Try.

THE SELECTIONS

4

Even Cowgirls Get the Blues by Tom Robbins

Paperback edition: Bantam Books, Inc., 1977

Chapter 15

Begins: Page 53: "Please don't think me immodest, but I'm really the best."

Ends: Page 55: "Maybe birds are stupid at that."

Suggested age and gender: Broad age range; male or female

Recommended for: REP, OB, DS, A

Summary

Sissy Hankshaw is a small-town gal from the honky-tonk tobacco fields of southern Virginia. She is outrageous! She is beautiful! She is adventurous! She is handicapped.

Born with an oversized set of thumbs ("They grew while she ate her grits and baloney; they grew while she slurped her Wheaties and milk"), there was little hope for anything else in life but to give herself completely to hitchhiking.

In this scene, Sissy has been given a truth serum by Dr. Goldman, one of several "specialists" she encountered (in hope of a cure), and tells of her hitchhiking triumphs.

Excerpt

Please don't think me immodest, but I'm really the best. When my hands are in shape and my timing is right, I'm the best there is, ever was or ever will be.

When I was younger, before this layoff that has nearly finished me, I hitchhiked one hundred and twenty-seven hours without stopping, without food or sleep, crossed the continent twice in six days, cooled my thumbs in both oceans and caught rides after midnight on unlighted highways, such was my skill, persuasion, rhythm. I set records and immediately cracked them; went farther, faster than any hitchhiker before or since. . . .

There is no road that did not expect me. Fields of daisies bowed and gas pumps gurgled when I passed by. Every moo cow dipped toward me her full udder. . . . I am the spirit and the heart of hitchhiking, I am its cortex and its medulla, I am its foundation and its culmination, I am the jewel in its lotus. And when I am really moving, stopping car after car after car, moving so freely, so clearly, so delicately that even the sex maniac and the cops can only blink and let me pass, then I embody the rhythms of the universe, I feel what it is like to *be* the universe, I am in a state of grace.

You may claim that I've an unfair advantage, but no more so than Nijinsky, whose reputation as history's most incomparable dancer is untainted by the fact that his feet were abnormal, having the bone structure of bird feet. Nature built Nijinsky to dance, me to direct traffic.

Treatment

• The dictionary defines *caricature* as a picture or description in which certain features or qualities are exaggerated or distorted to produce an absurd effect. It is tempting to make Sissy Hankshaw a caricature since the context of this material borders on the absurd. Make her a real person, with real feelings and needs. Taken seriously, the humor which is built into the text will emerge effortlessly. Have fun with this character as she is—vivacious, energetic, and colorful.

• The images in this piece are strong ones—for example, "Fields of daisies bowed and gas pumps gurgled when I passed by." The actor must substitute his or her own personal experiences to make these images spring to life. To find the reality of this character you have to examine your own life experiences and sensations. You may never have hitchhiked, but perhaps you remember skiing down a mountain at top speed, the beautiful snow and fresh air exhilarating your senses much the way Sissy becomes exhilarated when she is hitchhiking on the open road. The stronger the image(s) the more believable it becomes for you and your audience.

Working: People Talk About What They Do All Day and How They Feel About What They Do by Studs Terkel

Paperback edition: Avon Books, 1978

Book 5: "Footwork." Conrad Swibel

Begins: Page 365: "Reading gas meters, it's kind of a strenuous business."

Ends: Page 370: "It's to occupy your day, ya know? To pass the time of day."

Suggested age and gender: Broad age range; male

Recommended for: REP, OB, SS, DT, DS, A

Summary

Conrad Swibel, a gas meter reader from the Midwest, takes great pride in his work and meets each new day with vigor and a fine sense of humor.

Excerpt

Reading gas meters, it's kind of a strenuous business. . . . You have the blue shirt with the gas company on a patch. . . . They give you a badge with your ID picture. That helps you get in. They try to keep us on the same route so people will get used to you. People are suspicious.

I've been bit once already by a German shepherd. And that was something. It was really scary. It was an outside meter the woman had. I read the gas meter and was walking back out and heard a woman yell. I turned around and this German shepherd was comin' at me. The first thing I thought of was that he might go for my throat, like the movies. So I sort of crouched down and gave him my arm instead of my neck. He grabbed a hold of my arm, bit that, turned around. My arm was kinda soft, so I thought I'd give him something harder. So I gave him my hand. A little more bone in that. So he bit my hand.

. . . The big subject of conversation with us is dogs and women. . . . If you see a nice lady sitting there in a two-piece bathing suit—if you work it right and they'll be laying on their stomach in the sun and they'll have their top strap undone—if you go there and you scare 'em good enough, they'll jump up. To scare 'em where they jump up and you would be able to see them better, this takes time and it gives you something to do. . . .

Usually women follow you downstairs to make sure that maybe you're not gonna take nothin'. . .Of course, if she's wearing a nice short skirt, you follow her back up the stairs. (*Laughs*)

Treatment

• This is a simple, straightforward monologue. Conrad Swibel says exactly what he means and *tells* you how he feels about it. The actor needs to assume very little to interpret this character; the subtext is minimal: "I've been bitten once already by a German shepherd and that was something. It was really *scary*. . .[Almost every time you'll go into a house, they jump on you and sniff ya and if you do three hundred homes in a day, it gets *aggravating*."]

• Find the variety of the speech. Each tale Conrad tells "to pass the time of day" must be different from the next one. By attacking this character in the simplest, most obvious way, its many colors and textures will surface. An intensive, psychological investigation into the character's body and soul is probably unnecessary. Just go with it, and see what happens.

Working: People Talk About What They Do All Day and How They Feel About What They Do by Studs Terkel

Paperback edition: Avon Books, 1975

Book 5: "Footwork." Babe Secoli

Begins: Page 375: "We sell everything here. . .From potato chips and pop—we even have a genuine pearl in a can of oysters."

Ends: Page 380: "I look forward to comin' to work. I enjoy it somethin' terrible."

Suggested age and gender: Broad age range; female

Recommended for: REP, OB, SS, DT, DS, A

Summary

Babe Secoli is a supermarket checker and has known no other work. Babe delights in knowing she's a master at her craft, and would not change her position in life for anything. She embraces each day with competence, wit, arrogance, and zeal.

Excerpt

You sort of memorize the prices. It just comes to you. I know half a gallon of milk is sixty-four cents; a gallon, $1.10. You look at the labels. A small can of peas, Raggedy Ann. Green Giant, that's a few pennies more. I know Green Giant's eighteen and I know Raggedy Ann is fourteen. I know Del Monte is twenty-two. But lately the prices jack up from one day to another. Margarine two days ago was forty-three cents. Today it's forty-nine. Now when I see Imperial comin' through, I know it's forty-nine cents. You just memorize. One the register is a list of some prices, that's for the part-time girls. I never look at it.

I don't have to look at the keys on my register. I'm like the secretary that knows her typewriter. The touch. My hand fits. The number nine is my big middle finger. The thumb is number one, two and three and up. The side of my hand uses the bar for the total and all that.

I use my three fingers—my thumb, my index finger, and my middle finger. The right hand. And my left hand is on the groceries. They put down their groceries. I got my hips pushin' on the button and it rolls around on the counter. When I feel I have enough groceries in front of me, I let go of my hip. I'm just movin'—the hips, the hand, and the register, the hips, the hand, and the register. . .(*As she demonstrates, her hands and hips move in the manner of an Oriental dancer.*) You just keep goin', one, two, one, two. If you've got that rhythm, you're a fast checker. Your feet are flat on the floor and you're turning your head back and forth.

Somebody talks to you. If you take your hand off the item, you're gonna forget what you were ringin'. It's the feel. When I'm pushin' the items through I'm always having my hand on the items. If somebody interrupts to ask me the price, I'll answer while I'm movin'. Like playin' the piano.

Treatment

• To begin work on this character, observe various checkers at supermarkets in your neighborhood. This will give you a clearer picture of a typical day in the life of Babe Secoli. You may want to observe the following:

1. How do the checkers move?
2. How do they handle food?
3. How do they bag their groceries? (They all seem to have different techniques.)
4. Do they sit or stand?

• If given the opportunity, make "small talk" as your groceries are being checked. Learn as much as you can.

• Physicalize this character. The things she *does* are as important as how she feels about doing them. Observing "real life" situations can help in this process. Once you get the externals flowing, the internal needs of the character should surface with ease.

• Babe Secoli is intelligent, poignant, and alert.

American Dreams: Lost and Found by Studs Terkel

Hardcover edition: Pantheon Books, 1980 (also available in paper-
    back: Ballantine Books)

"Onward and Upward": Sharon Fox

Begins: Page 61: "I'm just one of millions."

Ends: Page 63: "If I can leave something behind creative, that
    I've done, maybe I'll be important to somebody."

Suggested age and gender: Broad age range; female

Recommended for: REP, OB, SS, DT, DS

Summary

Sharon Fox is a messenger at the Board of Trade in
Chicago. Her sideline is collecting autographs. Among her most
celebrated are those of Sylvester Stallone, Jack Ford, Yul Bryn-
ner, and Buster Crabbe.

She thinks of herself as a quiet, dull person. Collecting
autographs adds importance and glamour to her life. She is a
delightful personality: warm, endearing, and humorous.

Excerpt

I've grown up with these people, watching them on TV. I never
had many friends, so it was a substitute. I decided to go one
step further and meet these people instead of admiring them
from afar. My mother has an autographed picture of Jean Har-
low. So maybe it's in the genes somewhere. (*Laughs*)

I live at home. I never liked hanging out on street corners
or going to parties. I don't drink or smoke. We're a churchgo-
ing family, Baptist. My parents are all I've got, I'm all they've
got. They never had any hobbies. They have no real outside
interest, outside of me. They want to see me happy, and they're
interested in what I'm doing. Whatever I do reflects them.

They're like living through me. This is one country where you can do anything, and they prove it every day.

Are you familiar with Brenda Starr? I can identify with her. She's glamorous, not what I am. She's got this great love in her life, Basil St. John, which I don't have. She goes on all these exciting capers.

Treatment

• I cannot decide whether to laugh or cry at Sharon Fox. Perhaps that is the beauty of the speech. She claims to be a dull person, yet her experiences ("I met Prince Charles and he kissed me for my birthday") and attitudes ("If I can leave something behind creative, that I've done, maybe I'll be important to some-body") suggest otherwise. Perhaps the challenge of this speech is to work against that claim, concentrating on her humorous, passionate, and ingenuous qualities.

• Each experience she has triggers a different set of emotions and reactions. Make them bigger than they seem. On meeting Prince Charles she is not merely pleased but awestruck. On being sketched into the Brenda Starr comic strip, she is grateful and impressed.

• Sharon Fox is the kind of girl I would put at the top of my guest list and invite to a dull dinner party.

Letters from the Earth by Mark Twain; edited by Bernard DeVoto

Hardcover edition: Harper & Row Publishers, Inc., 1962 (also available in paperback: Harper & Row Publishers, Inc.)

"Letter II"

Begins: Page 8: "I have told you nothing about man that is not true."

Ends: Page 12: "He is a marvel—man is! I would I knew who invented him."

Suggested age and gender: Broad age range; male

Recommended for: OB, DS

Summary

In the guise of Satan, Mark Twain reports (to the archangels Gabriel and Michael) his observations on the "curious inhabitants of the planet Earth." He finds their ways and beliefs preposterous and astounding.

In Letter II, he describes man's invention of heaven: "It has invented a heaven. . . . guess what it is like! In fifteen hundred eternities you couldn't do it. The ablest mind known to you or me in fifty million aeons couldn't do it. Very well, I will tell you about it." He proceeds to do so in the style that has come to be known as vintage Twain: wildly funny, vigorous, and imaginative.

Excerpt

In man's heaven, EVERYBODY SINGS! The man who did not sing on earth sings there; the man who could not sing on earth is able to do it there. This universal singing is not casual, not occasional, not relieved by intervals of quiet; it goes on, all day long, and every day, during a stretch of twelve hours. And EVERYBODY STAYS; whereas in the earth the place would be empty in two hours. The singing is of hymns alone. Nay, it is of ONE hymn alone. The words are always the same, in number they are only about a dozen, there is no rhyme, there is no poetry: "Hosannah, hosannah, hosannah, Lord God of Sabaoth, (sic) 'rah! 'rah! 'rah! siss!-boom! . . .a-a-ah!"

Treatment

• One weekend, I found myself in Chapel Hill, North Carolina, with nothing to do. A friend told me Hal Holbrook was in town with his one-man show, "Mark Twain Tonight," and suggested I see it. The show prompted me to include this material among my selections. I found it to be very playable and wildly funny.

• Treat this piece as an artist would treat a blank canvas. Choose a persona or voice that suits your creative instincts. Twain suggests the guise of Satan as one possibility. But a more playable character might be an ex-priest turned flaming agnostic who in the style of an ambitious politician, must spread his views throughout the world. Try them both on for size.

• It would help to read as much Mark Twain as possible. Perhaps you can piece together material from other works. Hopefully, working in this manner will tempt you to research and compile works of other great writers. This is how one-man (-woman) shows are born. If you are a versatile performer, perhaps this is a direction in which you may want to go. Twain is a good place to start.

Catcher in the Rye by J. D. Salinger (not reproduced here)

Little, Brown & Company, 1945

Chapter 1

Begins: "If you really want to hear about it."

Ends: "If there's one thing I hate, it's the movies. Don't even mention them to me."

Suggested age and gender: Young; male

Recommended for: REP, OB, DS, A

Summary

Holden Caulfield is both the protagonist and the narrator of *Catcher In The Rye*, a chronicle of a sixteen-year-old boy who escapes to New York after flunking out of his third prep school.

In this opening scene, it is implied that Holden has had a nervous breakdown and speaks to us from an institution. ("I'll just tell you about this madman stuff that happened to me around last Xmas before I got pretty run-down and had to come out here and take it easy.") In a cry of mixed pain and pleasure, he unravels the memories of his "lousy childhood."

It is Holden's language that provides the dramatic excitement, the surprises, and the clues to his character. One learns about Holden not necessarily from his actions, but rather, from the way in which he expresses himself.

Treatment

• Read the entire book. If you have already done so, read it again. Try not to approach this piece from a literary point of view. That choice will not help you act it. Besides, you have already done that in high school English. Try to read the book as you would any dramatic script, looking for the answers to the following questions:

1. What is Holden's relationship to his parents, sister, brother, schoolmates, and so on?
2. What are his needs and demands in life?
3. What *would* make Holden happy?
4. What physical choices can be determined about him? How does he walk, run, shave, etc.?
5. What does his choice of language reveal?

• Be careful not to make this speech a one-note rendition of "Blues in the Night." Find the nuances, the different levels. Holden doesn't hate everything. Moments of pleasure and humor peep through his sarcasm and anger. It is almost as though he doesn't want to *get caught* feeling good about anything.

"Baby Gets a Tattoo" by Deanne Stillman

The Village Voice, October 21–27, 1981

This selection appears in its entirety.

Also by Deanne Stillman: *Getting Back at Dad,* Wideview Books, 1981

Suggested age and gender: Broad age range; male or female

Recommended for: REP, OB, SS, DS

Summary

After much anxiety about getting a tattoo, the character in this piece heads for Woodstock, New York in pursuit of renowned tattoo artist Spider Webb. Despite overhearing horrifying screams (another subject being tattooed) in the waiting room of Spider's tattoo cottage, the character courageously endures, and in the end acquires a lovely tattoo in a very secret place.

Excerpt

Don't tell my mom that I have a tattoo because she'll probably kill me. She says you can't be buried in a Jewish cemetery if you have a tattoo, and even if you could, Jews shouldn't do cheap things like painting their bodies (permanently). Only sailors and marines and stevedores who get drunk and stumble into cheap parlors in places like Hong Kong and the waterfront of Cleveland get tattoos, not Jews. So don't tell my mom, okay?

The tattoo that I got is really neat. I'm sorry, but I can't tell you what it looks like or even where it is because it's supposed to be a surprise for the people who get to see it. In other words, it's not on my right or left arm, or my neck, or my feet. (Hint: it's not on my thighs, either.)

I got the tattoo the day after some people with a crowbar pried off the door to my loft and ripped me off. Here's what they took: two gold necklaces and an amethyst ring and two strings of pearls my grandmother gave me before she died. All the jewelry had street and sentimental value. They also took a gram of cocaine and left me one line. That turned out to be a good thing because it gave me enough energy to call the police. My friend Bob arrived first and surveyed the scene of the crime. (Bob has a tattoo too; it's a small one and you can hardly see it, but his mom noticed it one day, and she got mad.) Bob said, "It's time for a piece of jewelry no one can steal."

I had been thinking about getting a tattoo for a long time, but I never looked at it that way. So Bob and I went to Woodstock to visit our friend Spider Webb, known in tattoo circles as the best tattoo artist in the tri-state area, if not the whole world. I told him what I wanted and where I wanted it and he said to think about it overnight and if I still wanted it the next day, I should come back.

I thought about it all night, which is what I had been doing for months, but it seemed like a good idea to think about it one more time. I thought about all the reasons I shouldn't get a tattoo. First of all, I thought about how mad my mom would get. Would I be rejected by a Jewish cemetery? Then I thought about how I might not like the tattoo next week. Then I worried about how much it would hurt to get the tattoo. Then I thought that certain people would think I was copying Janis Joplin, even though it was about 15 years later. Then I thought some people would think I was getting a tattoo just because of that new Bruce Dern movie called *Tattoo*. And then I thought about how mad my mom would get. Would she tell me to go join a circus?

I didn't care. I wanted to become a member of the world's oldest cult. I wanted to partake of a ritual that knows no national boundaries. I wanted to have a piece of art that I could always wear. I wanted a permanent decoration, something that would look great with everything. I wanted to surprise my friends and confuse my enemies. Also, I was pretty drunk.

I went back to Spider Webb's the next day. His place is not a tattoo parlor, it's a tattoo cottage. He says that if you want the kind of tattoo you get in a tattoo parlor, you should go down the street to the local tattoo parlor, where the guy outlines all his tattoos in black ink. Spider's place is right near the Woodstock town green, next to a place that does ear-piercing. If you really want to make your mom mad, you could stop there after you get your tattoo.

While you're waiting for Spider, you can sit on a couch and read his book, *Pushing Ink*. It says that Jennie Churchill and Barry Goldwater have tattoos, something that may convince you to either stay or leave, depending on your point of view. It also says, "The tattoo will let you know if it wants you, and where."

When I arrived, Spider was finishing up another tattoo. I heard a woman's screams coming from the room where he was working. I knocked on the door and asked if I could take a peek. No one seemed to mind. In fact, the woman seemed excited that someone wanted to witness her screams. Spider was carefully tattooing a long-stemmed rose on the woman's foot. It covered a scar. The tattoo was truly beautiful, a perpetual blossom climbing up from between two toes. Every time Spider applied the needle, the woman shrieked. And this was only her foot! I started to panic.

Spider soon emerged. I asked why the woman screamed so much. "Some people are screamers," he said, and smiled. Then he asked me if I still wanted my tattoo. I said yes. He said he thought that I still did, and last night had drawn a special design based on my description of the tattoo I wanted. It was beautiful—but about three inches too big.

Spider likes to work big because that's the way he thinks. I asked him to scale it down and he asked me again if I really wanted the tattoo. I said yes. He smiled and scaled it down. When the size was right, I went inside his studio and he went to work.

I won't go into all the details because it might scare you. And I don't want to do that because a tattoo is definitely something worth getting if you really want one. I will say that it hurt. I'm not a screamer so I didn't scream. But I think I invented several dozen words consisting of consonants during the two-hour-long session. I will also say that if anyone can make getting a tattoo a pleasure, it's Spider Webb.

That's because Spider Webb is like Groucho Marx on angel dust. A Zen Rodney Dangerfield. Captain Kangaroo with an electric needle. If Spider had his own TV show, the announcer would say, "Kids, Spider Webb is a professional. Check with mom before trying to imitate Spider. . ." Spider Webb looks like the kind of guy who has a secret. And he does. He tells you his secret through the colors that he carefully pushes under your skin. He inserts a needle flowing with red ink. "You know what they say," he says. I'm splayed out in pain. "What?"

"A fool and his money are soon parted." And then Spider Webb laughs, as if sharing a private joke with the ancients. Is this what Egyptian tattoo artists told Cleopatra when she had reached the point of no return?

My tattoo is all healed now, and it's the nicest piece of art that I have. If you know Spider Webb's work, you know it looks like a Spider Webb tattoo. I unveiled it a couple of weeks ago, and my friends wanted to know where I got it and how much it cost. (Spider's prices start at $50.) No one mentioned Janis Joplin or Bruce Dern. A couple of people mentioned the Stones' new album, "Tattoo You."

Well, at least they can't call me chicken. And when I walk down the street, I know there must be a lot of people, maybe as many as the number that live in Pennsylvania, who have tattoos that only their closest friends know about. I know that there are a lot of people who have jewelry that no one can steal. It's a feeling I get. Spider says that sometimes you can just tell when someone has a tattoo.

But don't tell my mom, okay?

Treatment

I share the following notes which were taken while watching an actress audition with this monologue.

1. I enjoyed the actress enjoying herself. This speech has great comic potential. She subtly captured its off-beat humor without pushing for laughs.

2. The story seemed to roll off her tongue as though she had *recently* experienced it. There was a sense of excitement and immediacy to her delivery.

3. The piece was well edited.

4. I travelled with her on a journey which began in fear ("Please don't tell my mom") and insecurity (". . .When I arrived, Spider was finishing up another tattoo. I heard a woman's screams coming from the room where he was working.") and ended with feelings of relief and satisfaction.

Lady Oracle by Margaret Atwood (not reproduced here)

Simon & Schuster, 1976

Chapter 5

Begins: Page 42: "My Mother named me after Joan Crawford."

Ends: Page 51: "Besides, who would think of marrying a moth-
ball?"

Suggested age and gender: Broad age range; female

Recommended for: REP, OB, SS, DT, DS, A

Summary

Among other imperfections, Joan Foster was a grossly
overweight child. She kept a photograph of herself on a dresser,
but when asked about it, claimed it was that of a favorite aunt.
She managed to conceal this secret and many others (she wrote
Gothic romances under a pseudonym) throughout her adult life.

In this piece she describes the many ways her disapprov-
ing mother tried to deal with her daughter's shortcomings. "When
I was eight or nine my Mother would look at me and say mus-
ingly, "To think that I named you after Joan Crawford!" She goes
on to describe how Mother, hoping to make Joan less chubby,
enrolled her in Miss Flegg's dancing school, where she performed
such memorable routines as "Tulip Time," "Anchors Aweigh,"
and "The Butterfly Frolic."

It is this particular memory, and the author's detailed
description of it, that provide a monologue of wit, compassion,
and sentiment.

Treatment

See Treatment from *Working* (Conrad Swibel), *American Dreams: Lost and Found* and *California and Other States
of Grace.*

"Popping Up in 60 Minutes" by Russell Baker (not reproduced here)

New York Times Magazine, Sunday Observer Column, March 2, 1980 (also available on microfilm)

Begins: "In my first dream about appearing on *60 Minutes*, Harry Reasoner did the interviewing."

Ends: "If Tom Snyder refuses to take my case, it's curtains."

Suggested age and gender: Broad age range; male or female

Recommended for: REP, OB, SS, DT, DS, A

Summary

In this piece the narrator dreams that the *60 Minutes* crew has asked him to appear on their television show for an interview. They wish to interrogate him about his faulty toaster. In the course of the piece he finds the members of the *60 Minutes* news team in different rooms of his house.

Morley Safer explains that the team is doing an exposé on people who waste energy: "Poets who burn the midnight oil. . .condemned murderers who insist on being electrocuted instead of hanged." He goes on to say they are now interested in the character's toasting habits.

Dan Rather discovers that the toaster has to be warmed up before it will toast the bread. He asks, "Is is not a fact that you prefer to keep this ancient, outmoded toaster which is so dilapidated that the toast has to be pushed down, not just once, but twice?" In a fit of paranoia, the character seizes the toaster, rushes into the bedroom, slams the door, only to hear:

"True or False?" The voice is familiar. "You are a toaster batterer." It is none other than Mike Wallace.

In despair, the character pleads guilty, throwing himself on the mercy of Shana Alexander and James Kilpatrick.

Treatment

See Treatment from *Working* (Conrad Swibel and Babe Secoli). In addition: your reaction to each confrontation and to each interviewer must vary. The speech begins with the most amiable interviewer. You are relaxed and confident. You move on to the next interviewer—paranoia sets in. You are at last confronted with the most vicious of the three interviewers. By this time you are a vision of pathos and frenzy, begging for mercy from anyone who can help you. As the "plot" progresses, the comedy builds.

Getting Even by Woody Allen

Paperback edition: Warner Paperback Library (published by arrangement with Random House, Inc.)

"A Little Louder Please"

Begins: Page 82: "On the night of the performance, the two of us—I in my opera cape and Lars with his pail—."

Ends: Page 84: "I don't like to be bothered once I'm asleep."

Suggested age and gender: Broad age range; male

Recommended for: SS, DT

Summary

This gentleman has been plagued since childhood by his inability to understand the art of pantomime.

In this piece, he and Lars (his window-washer) attend a pantomime entitled, *Going to a Picnic.* His "mimetic shortcomings" are enhanced and his confusion thickens as he struggles to interpret the performance.

Excerpt

The mime now proceeded to spread a picnic blanket, and instantly my old confusion set in. He was either spreading a picnic blanket or milking a small goat. Next, he elaborately removed his shoes, except that I'm not positive they were his shoes because he drank one of them and mailed the other to Pittsburgh. I say "Pittsburgh," but actually it is hard to mime the concept of Pittsburgh, and as I look back on it, I now think what he was miming was not Pittsburgh at all but a man driving a golf cart through a revolving door or possibly two men dismantling a printing press.

Treatment

• See Treatment from *The Grass Is Always Greener Over the Septic Tank* and *Even Cowgirls Get the Blues.*

• In addition: The difficulty of this piece is in creating a believable, three-dimensional character. By doing so you voyage one step beyond the comedy routine and into a character an audience can empathize and identify with.

The Grass Is Always Greener Over the Septic Tank by **Erma Bombeck** (not reproduced here)

Hardcover edition: McGraw-Hill Book Company, 1976 (also available in paperback: Crest/Fawcett)

Chapter 7: "It Comes with the Territory"—Loneliness

Begins: Page 91: "No one talked about it a lot, but everyone knew what it was."

Ends: Page 98: "By the way, could you call and let me know how Lisa makes out on *As The World Turns*."

Suggested age and gender: Middle-aged; female

Recommended for: SS, DT

Summary

While chatting over a cup of coffee with neighbor Helen, our character reveals a case of the housewife blues. Boredom and restlessness abound. The symptoms are evident: "The other day I flushed a Twinkie down the toilet just to please Jack LaLanne." She goes on to confess: "I would have graduated from college this June. That's right. If I had just found my car keys, I could have picked up my B.A. and could be one of those women who only wash on Saturdays and freeze their bread."

As with all the writings of Erma Bombeck, humor and sarcasm prevail.

Treatment

• You may wish to perform this material as a stand-up comedy routine. It certainly is appropriate for cabaret shows or nightclub acts. If you choose to treat it as a comedy routine, keep in mind that the primary intention should be to entertain.

• I have also seen actors build real characters from this material. The character is obvious: a frustrated middle-class housewife who longs to be upwardly mobile and respected. The humor lies in her *failure* to get the things she wants.

Aunt Erma's Cope Book by **Erma Bombeck** (not reproduced here)

Hardcover edition: McGraw-Hill Book Company, 1979 (also available in paperback: Crest/Fawcett)

Chapter 9: "The Complete Book of Jogging"

Begins: Page 75: "Jim Fixit's legs were the first thing I saw every morning and the last thing I saw every night."

Ends: Page 83: "Easy for Mr. Fixit."

Suggested age and gender: Broad age range; male or female

Recommended for: SS, DT

Summary

One can hardly call Aunt Erma a physical fitness enthusiast. Mere contemplation of such activities makes her wince. Eventually she is plunged into the world of jogging by family and friends and endures their boasts of blisters, shin splints, back pains and Achilles tendonitis. They speak "fluent jogging" (e.g., "euphoria," "building up lactic acid") while she cringes at the very thought of the sport.

It was only a matter of time before her "inner peace had brought out her outer fat." With a $65.00 pink velour warm-up suit in hand, she joins the masses and converts.

Treatment

See Treatment from *The Grass Is Always Greener Over the Septic Tank.*

The Art of Ruth Draper: Her Dramas and Characters
   by Morton Dauwen Zabel
Hardcover edition: Doubleday, Inc., 1960
"A Scottish Immigrant at Ellis Island."
Begins: Page 136: "Goodbye, Annie. Goodbye. . ."
Ends: Page 139: "Sandy! My Sandy. . .I'm here!"
Suggested age and gender: Young (19–27); female
Recommended for: DS

Summary

Leslie MacGregor is a young girl from the Highlands of Scotland who has just arrived at Ellis Island in New York harbor, the point of entry for immigrants coming to the United States. Leslie has come to meet her prospective husband whom she has not seen for three years.

Excerpt

Good morning, sir—good morning. . .My name?. . .Leslie MacGregor. . .Leslie. . .L-E-S-L-I-E. . .That's all. . .It is. My only name. . .Just Leslie. It's a Scottish name. . .I come from Crianlarich. . .Crianlarich. It's a small place—it's part way between Loch Katrine and Loch Awe in the Highlands of Scotland. . .Spell it?. . .Ye spell it C-R-I-A-N-L-A-R-I-C-H. Crianlarich. . .

I'm twenty-one years old. . .I have come oot to mary. . . Oh, he's here. . .Oh, yes. I know 'im. . .His name?. . .His name is Mr. Alexander MacAllister. . .

Well, d'ye see—he left home three years ago, and when he had enough, he was to send for me. So now I have come. . .Aye, he knows I'm coming. . .He'll be here the day to meet me. I'm sure he will. . .I beg your pardon?. . .Polygamist—am I a polygamist? What ever is that?. . .Am I married?. . .Oh, no, Sir—I'm not married. . .Anarchist? Is that a religion?. . .I am a Presbyterian. . .In prison? Have I been to prison? No, Sir—we have no prison in Crianlarich. . .Asylum? De ye mean where the puir daft people go?. . .No, Sir—we have no asylum in Crianlarich. . .Contagious diseases? Well, I had a cold on the steamer coming over, but it's gone now—would that be a contagious disease?. . .No, Sir—I've never been ill; only in the wintertime, sometimes I have a wee cold! Come out under contract?. . .No contract—only to Mr. MacAllister!

Treatment

• It would be both appropriate and effective to use a stage dialect with this character. As I note in the audition guidelines (see Dialects, page 00), you should rehearse the piece in your own speech, tagging the dialect on last. Perhaps this selection is best suited for an exercise in an acting or voice class. To help build this character, ask yourself the following questions:

1. Where have I come from? (her past)
2. What are my expectations about America?
3. What are my expectations of Alexander MacAllister?
4. How do you pronounce "Crianlarich"?

• You may wish to stage this speech as a scene rather than a monologue. To capture Leslie MacGregor's innocence, excitement, and confusion, it could be helpful to have the clerk present.

The Art of Ruth Draper: Her Dramas and Characters
   by Morton Dauwen Zabel
Hardcover edition: Doubleday, Inc., 1960
"The German Governess"
Begins: Page 165: "Quiet, please, children!. . .And go to your places. . ."
Ends: Page 168: ". . .Ich kann's nicht langer aushalten. . ."
Suggested age and gender: Middle-aged; female
Recommended for: DS

Summary

"She sits in a straight chair before her pupils in the classroom of their family home. . .worn and harassed by her years of teaching, and nervously aware of her unruly charges."

Excerpt

Now, children, I am going to read you a beautiful little poem!. . .One minute! Harry—get up from under the desk there! What have you got in your blouse?. . .What?. . .Guinea pigs?. . .Those baby guinea pigs?. . .Children, where do you get these ideas? There is absolutely nothing funny about it—it is outrageous! Cruelty to animals!. . .Now, children, please turn to page sixty-six. You will enjoy this. It is a very famous poem called "Die Lorelei."

Ich weiss nich, was soll es bedeuten,
Dass ich so traurig bin;
Ein Marchen aus alten Zeiten,
Das kommt mir nicht aus dem Sinn.

Who threw this dead fly? Who threw it?. . .Children—I can't stand it any longer! I come here every morning—I give you my life and my time. I try so hard to make you happy, and I have only insults. I will control myself, now—but mind you—you will hear of this again. It is by no means the end— your parents shall hear of it! It's outrageous!"

Treatment

See Treatment from: *The Art of Ruth Draper:* "Scottish Immigrant."

California and Other States of Grace by Phyllis Theroux

Hardcover edition: William Morrow & Company, Inc., 1980 (also available in paperback: Fawcett Books)

Chapter V

Begins: Page 94: "When I turned nine and it was discovered that I needed glasses, Hollywood and stardom were not in my line of vision."

Ends: Page 103: "All my glossies would be accompanied by personal, handwritten notes."

Suggested age and gender: Young; female

Recommended for: REP, OB, SS, DT, DS, A

Summary

Struggling with childhood self-doubts and determined to escape a life of "lukewarm obscurity," the author finds in her idol, Margaret O'Brien, a Hollywood fantasy that eases the growing pains.

In this selection, she reflects upon those childhood memories.

Excerpt

When I turned nine and it was discovered that I needed glasses, Hollywood and stardom were not in my line of vision. I vaguely knew about Margaret O'Brien (my parents had taken me to see *Little Women* for my eighth birthday), but it was not until the day I sat waiting for my eyes to dilate in a doctor's office and listened to my mother read aloud from a book entitled something like "Margaret O'Brien's Very Own Diary"— not until that moment did I realize what stale doughnuts I had been eating all those years. My God, what a life that girl was leading. . .!

My heart stretched with envy. That I should be wearing dresses from Macy's Chubette Department and be 3,000 miles from an Automat. That I should be holding soggy tomato sandwiches in a hot schoolyard while Margaret was holding press conferences and getting toy Collies from unknown admirers. What kind of God was this who would visit astigmatism and flyaway hair upon the head of one nine-year-old and bestow twenty-twenty vision and a set of shiny black braids upon another? In one moment which extended for the next several years, I decided that Margaret O'Brien did not deserve her life. Wondering why I fixated upon Margaret O'Brien and not Shirley Temple, I think the reason was twofold: Shirley Temple was too treacly for my tastes. Secondly, Margaret O'Brien might be easier to knock off.

Treatment

• See Treatment from *Even Cowgirls Get the Blues*, *Working* (Conrad Swibel), and *American Dreams: Lost and Found.*
In addition: This speech is a child's fantasy—delicate and heartwarming. The insecurity and confusion which accompanies adolescence is an important part of the piece. The character yearns to be someone else ("my heart stretched with envy"), certain her own life is insignificant and mundane.

• Like so many monologues in this book, *California and Other States of Grace* is a stroll down memory lane. It is only in retrospect that the memories are humorous. While they were being lived, they were painful and frightening.

The Portable Dorothy Parker (revised and enlarged edition) (not reproduced here)

Paperback edition: Viking Press, 1973

"The Waltz"

Begins: Page 47: "Why, thank you so much. I'd adore to."

Ends: Page 51: "I'd simply adore to go on waltzing."

Suggested age and gender: Broad age range; female

Recommended for: REP, OB, SS, DT, DS, A

Summary

Here we are at the dance. The character cringes at the prospect of being asked to dance by a gentleman she suspects is an idiot. It turns out he is graced with the dancing skills of "Mrs. O'Leary's cow."

"What can you say, when a man asks you to dance with him? 'I most certainly will NOT dance with you, I'll see you in hell first. Why, thank you, I'd like to awfully, but I'm having labor pains. Oh, yes, do let's dance together—it's so nice to meet a man who isn't a scaredy-cat about catching my beri-beri!"

Reluctantly she accepts his invitation. Her inner monologue continues while waltzing with the gentleman, who by this time has managed to kick her in the shins, crush her instep and shove her against the wall.

Treatment

• As with all the writings of Dorothy Parker, her prose is humorous, bright, and sharp-edged. The characters are pathetic little creatures who blame God (and everyone else) for life's injustices. ("Why can't he let me lead my own life? I ask so little—just to be left alone in my quiet corner of the table, to do my evening brooding over all my sorrows.")

• While developing these characters, take note of their two contrasting levels. On the surface, they are witty, charming, and sincere. ("Oh, yes, it's a waltz. Mind? Why, simply thrilled. I'd love to waltz with you.") These niceties are cover-ups for the character's real feelings and needs. Anger and frustration lie beneath the surface and reveal the true identities of these women. ("I'd love to waltz with you, I'd love to have my tonsils out, I'd love to be in a midnight fire at sea.")

• It should be easy to connect and identify with these characters since their problems are universal. We (especially women) have experienced these predicaments at least once in our lives. Perhaps this is the attraction of Dorothy Parker's characters.

The Portable Dorothy Parker (revised and enlarged edition) (not reproduced here)

Paperback edition: Viking Press, 1973

"The Little Hours"

Begins: Page 254: "Now what's this? What's the object of all this darkness all over me?"

Ends: Page 259: ". . .Till the next ten o'clock, if I feel like it."

Suggested age and gender: Broad age range; male or female

Recommended for: REP, OB, SS, DT, DS, A

Summary

"At the time when all decent people are just going to bed, I must wake."

At four-thirty A.M. we find the character in "The Little Hours" plagued with insomnia. She (or he) takes us on a journey of frustrating attempts to drift back to sleep. When reading fails, she tries counting sheep. "I hate sheep. . .I can tell the minute one's in the room. They needn't think that I am going to lie here in the dark and count their unpleasant little faces for them."

When counting sheep fails, she finally decides to make a list of beautiful and profound quotations: "To thine own self be true." "If winter comes, can spring be far behind?" "Mrs. Porter and her daughter wash their feet in soda water." Et cetera.

The prose in "The Little Hours" abounds with wit and sarcasm. It is quite appropriate for either sex.

Treatment

See Treatment from *The Portable Dorothy Parker:* "The Waltz."

The Portable Dorothy Parker (revised and enlarged edition) (not reproduced here)

Paperback edition: Viking Press, 1973

"Sentiment"

Begins: Page 354. "Oh, anywhere, driver, anywhere—it doesn't matter. Just keep driving."

Ends: Page 359. "Driver, what street is this? Sixty-Fifth? Oh. No. nothing, thank you. I—I thought it was Sixty-Third. . ."

Suggested age and gender: Broad age range; female

Recommended for: REP, OB, SS, DT, DS, A

Summary

In an attempt to mend a broken heart, Rosalie seeks refuge in a taxi cab (where the entire scene takes place). She has no particular destination and instructs the driver to "just keep driving." It's better than walking. If she was walking she might catch a glimpse of her former lover in the crowded street: "Someone with his swing of the shoulders, his slant of the hat."

As she continues to be driven aimlessly throughout the city she talks herself through the stages of their now ill-fated romance. These thoughts are soon interrupted when she screams to the driver not to ride through a particular street. "This was our street, this is the place of our love and laughter." Rosalie proceeds to crouch down below the back seat with her hands tightly covering her eyes. "Oh why can't I be let to die as we pass through?"

As in "The Little Hours" and "The Waltz," "Sentiment" is deliciously witty and sarcastic.

Treatment

See Treatment from: "The Waltz," page 57.

Les Liaisons Dangereuses **by Choderlos de Laclos**

Letter 97

1782, Paris

This piece appears in its entirety.

Suggested age and gender: Broad age range; female

Recommended for: REP, OB, DS

Summary

Les Liaisons Dangereuses is a series of letters (175) which describes two ruthless aristocrats, the Marquise de Merteuil and the Vicomte de Valmont and their scheme to seduce a young girl, Cécile Volanges.

In this scene, Cécile tells Madame de Merteuil the guilt and shame felt after Monsieur de Valmont seduced her. She blames herself for not protesting the act and allowing him to return the next evening. "I was so very agitated! If it is always as difficult as this to defend oneself, one needs a good deal of practice!"

LETTER 97: CÉCILE VOLANGES TO THE
MARQUISE DE MERTEUIL

OH God, Madame, how heavy-hearted, how miserable I am! Who will console me in my distress? Who will advise me in my difficulties? This Monsieur de Valmont . . . and Danceny? No: the very thought of Danceny throws me into despair. . . . How shall I tell you? How shall I say it? . . . I dont' know what to do. But my heart is full . . . I must speak to someone, and in you alone can I, dare I confide. You have been so kind to me! What shall I say? I do not want you to be kind. Everyone here has offered me sympathy to-day . . . they have only increased my wretchedness: I was so very much aware that I did not deserve it! Scold me instead; give me a good scolding, for I am very much to blame. But then save me. If you will not have the kindness to advise me I shall die of grief.

Know then . . . my hand trembles, as you see. I can scarcely write. I feel my cheeks on fire. . . . Oh, it is the very blush of shame. Well, I shall endure it. It shall be the first punishment for my fault. Yes, I shall tell you everything.

You must know, then, that Monsieur de Valmont who hitherto has delivered Monsieur Danceny's letters to me, suddenly found it too difficult to continue in the usual way. He wanted a key to my room. I can certainly assure you that I did not want to give him one: but he went so far as to write to Danceny, and Danceny wanted me to do so. I am always so sorry to refuse him anything, particularly since our separation which has made him so unhappy, that I finally agreed. I had no idea of the misfortune that would follow.

Last night Monsieur de Valmont used the key to come into my room as I slept. I was so little expecting this that he really frightened me when he woke me. But as he immediately began to speak, I recognized him and did not cry out; then, too, it occurred to me at first that he had come to bring me a letter from Danceny. Far from it. Very shortly afterwards he attempted to kiss me; and while I defended myself, as was natural, he cleverly did what I should not have wished for all the world. . .but first he wanted a kiss. I had to: what else could I do? The more so since I had tried to ring, but besides the fact that I could not, he was careful to tell me that if someone came he would easily be able to throw all the blame on me; and, in fact, it would have been easy on account of the key. After this he budged not an inch. He wanted a second kiss; and, I don't know why, but this time I was quite flustered and afterwards it was even worse than before. Oh, really, it was too wicked. Then, after that. . .you will spare my telling you the rest, but I am as unhappy as anyone could possibly be.

What I blame myself for most, and what, nevertheless, I must tell you about, is that I am afraid I did not defend myself as well as I was able. I don't know how that happened. I most certainly am not in love with Monsieur de Valmont, quite the contrary: yet there were moments when it was as if I were. . . .As you may imagine, this did not prevent me from saying no all the time: but I knew quite well that I was not doing as I said: it was as if I could not help it. And then, too, I was so very agitated! If it is always as difficult as this to defend oneself, one needs a good deal of practice! It is true that Monsieur de Valmont has a way of saying things so that one is hard put to it to think of a reply: at all events, would you believe that when he left I was almost sorry, and was weak enough to agree to his returning this evening? That is what horrifies me more than all the rest.

Oh, in spite of all, I promise you I shall stop him coming. He had scarcely left when I knew for certain that I had been very wrong to promise him anything. What is more, I spent the rest of the night in tears. It was Danceny above all who haunted me! Every time I thought of him my tears came twice as fast till they almost suffocated me, and I thought of him all the time. . . .I do even now, and you see the result: my paper quite sodden. No, I shall never be consoled, if only on his account. . . .At length I could cry no more, and yet could not sleep for a minute. And when I woke this morning and looked at myself in the mirror, I frightened myself, I was so changed.

Mamma noticed it as soon as she saw me, and asked me what was wrong. I began at once to cry. I thought she was going to scold me, and perhaps that would have hurt me less: but quite the contrary. She spoke to me kindly! I scarcely deserved it. She told me not to distress myself like that! She did not know what I had to be distressed about. She said that I would make myself ill! There are moments when I should like to be dead. I could not restrain myself. I threw myself sobbing into her arms, crying 'Oh, Mamma your daughter is very unhappy!' Mamma could not help crying a little herself, and that only increased my misery. Fortunately she did not ask why I was unhappy, or I would not have known what to say.

I beseech you, Madame, write to me as soon as you can and tell me what I must do; for I have not the courage to think of anything and can do nothing but suffer. Please address your letter to Monsieur de Valmont; but if you are writing to him at the same time, I beg you not to mention that I have said anything to you.

I have the honour to be, Madame, ever with the most sincere friendship, your very humble and obedient servant. . . .I dare not sign this letter.

Château de—
1 October 17—

Treatment

• The background of this book is rather interesting. When it was first published in 1782 French society was outraged

63

and it caused quite a scandal. It is said that "young ladies would retire with it behind locked doors." It was later found in the library of Marie-Antoinette.

In 1824, the government condemned it to be a work of "revolting immorality, a book to be admired and execrated."

• The piece easily transforms into a monologue. The young girl does not have to be writing a letter to Madame de Merteuil. You can change the situation to suit your needs. i.e. Cécile pays a visit to the home of Madame and begins the speech there. This seems a more "actable" choice than writing a letter and allows for more physical movement and interaction with another character.

• The piece runs a bit long and you will most likely have to edit. See Chapter I, "How to Use This Book," to help in the process.

• There are 175 letters to choose from in *Les Liaisons Dangereuses* which are spoken by characters other than Cécile Volanges. The letters of Valmont, Merteuil, and Danceny (male) adapt well to monologue form.

Sophie's Choice by **William Styron**

Paperback edition: Bantam Books, 1980 (by arrangement with Random House, Inc.)

Chapter 13

This selection appears in its entirety.

Suggested age and gender: Broad age range; female

Recommended for: REP, OB

Summary

Wanda is a prisoner in the women's compound at Birkenau during the Nazi Occupation. In this scene she finds her way to Sophie's side and "through a tumultuous outpouring" fills Sophie with hope about her son Jan and the possibility that he is safe and well.

Wanda passionately pleads with Sophie to *use* her position as translator-stenographer to the German Commandant, Rudolph Höss, to liberate her son and further the cause of the Resistance.

Excerpt

I knew I had to see you when I heard about you through the grapevine. We hear everything. I've so wanted to see you anyway all these months, but this new job of yours made it absolutely necessary. I've risked everything to get here to see you—if I'm caught I'm done for! But nothing risked, nothing gained in this snakepit. Yes, I'll tell you again and believe me: Jan is well, he's as well as can be expected. Yes, not once—three times I saw him through the fence. I won't fool you, he's skinny as I am. It's lousy in the Children's Camp—everything's lousy at Birkenau—but I'll tell you another thing. They're not starving the children as badly as some of the rest. Why, I don't know, it can't be their conscience. Once I managed to take him some apples. He's doing well. He can make it. Go ahead and cry, darling, I know it's awful but you mustn't give up hope. And you've got to try to get him out of here before winter comes. Now, this *Lebensborn idea may sound bizarre but the thing really exists—we saw it happening in Warsaw, remember the Rydzón child?—and I'm telling you that you simply must make a stab at using it to get Jan shipped out of here. All right, I know there's a good chance that he might get lost if he's sent to Germany, but at least he'll be alive and well, don't you see? There's a good chance that you'll be able to keep track of him, this war can't last forever.

Listen! It all depends on what kind of relationship you strike up with Höss. So much depends on that, Zosia darling, not only what happens to Jan and yourself but to all of us. You've got to *use* that man, work on him—you're going to be living under the same roof. Use him! For once you've got to forget that priggish Christer's morality of yours and use your sex for all it's worth. . .Listen, underground intelligence knows all about that man, just as we've learned about Lebensborn. Höss is just another susceptible bureaucrat with a blocked-up itch for a female body. Use it! And use him! It won't be any skin off his nose to take one Polish kid and have him committed to that program—after all, it'll be another bonus for the Reich. And sleeping with Höss won't be collaboration, it'll be espionage—a fifth column! Zosia, this is your chance! What you do in that house can mean everything for the rest of us, for every Pole and Jew and misbegotten bundle of misery in this camp—*everything*. I beg of you—don't let us down!

Treatment

Wanda's character is well described in this excerpt from *Sophie's Choice:*

". . . .She had a vivacity, a luminous intensity which sometimes transformed her in a spectacular way; she glowed, she

---

*The wholesale kidnapping of foreign children to add to the breeding stock of the Third Reich. On Heinrich Himmler's orders children with Aryan-looking features were selected in mass examinations, brought to Germany for placement in indoctrination centers, and then put up for adoption by "racially trustworthy" German families.

became all sparks and fire (Sophie often thought of the word *fougueuse*) like her hair.

. . . .Sophie never believed that such violent patriotism could dwell within a human breast, even in a land of throbbing patriots. Wanda was the reincarnation of the young Rosa Luxemburg, whom she worshipped. She seldom mentioned her father, nor did she ever try to explain why she had rejected so completely the German part of her heritage; Sophie only knew that Wanda breathed, drank and dreamed of a free Poland—most radiantly, a liberated Polish proletariat after the war—and such a passion had turned her into one of the most unbudgingly committed members of the Resistance. She was sleepless, fearless, clever—a firebrand."

For the Term of His Natural Life by Marcus Clarke

Lloyd O'Neil Pty. Ltd. Victoria, Australia (also published in London, America, and Germany)

1869

Book Four, chapter 67: "Diary of the Rev. James North"

This piece appears in its entirety.

Suggested age and gender: Broad age range; male

Recommended for: REP, DS

Summary

In 1846, James North spent 7 years as the Protestant chaplain of a penal colony off the coast of Sydney, Australia. He was assigned the post to establish order and discipline amongst the prisoners of the colony.

He once thought of himself as a college-hero, prizeman, poet, and man of deep religious ideals. Rev. North comes to realize he is no longer the man he once was. In this scene he struggles with his conscience and begs God to forgive him for having sinned. He has been tempted by love and lust for a woman and cannot bear the guilt and shame.

He makes a final plea to be pitied and forgiven or else be allowed to die.

Excerpt

EXTRACTED FROM THE DIARY OF
THE REV. JAMES NORTH

December 7th.—I have made up my mind to leave this place, to bury myself again in the bush, I suppose, and await extinction. I try to think that the reason for this determination is the frightful condition of misery existing among the prisoners; that because I am daily horrified and sickened by scenes of torture and infamy, I decide to go away; that, feeling myself powerless to save others, I wish to spare myself. But in this journal, in which I bind myself to write nothing but truth, I am forced to confess that these are *not* the reasons. I will write the reason plainly: "I covet my neighbour's wife." It does not look well thus written. It looks hideous. In my own breast I find numberless excuses for my passion. I said to myself, "My neighbour does not love his wife, and her unloved life is misery. She is forced to live in the frightful seclusion of this accursed island, and she is dying for want of companionship. She feels that I understand and appreciate her, that I could love her as she deserves, that I could render her happy. I feel that I have met the only woman who has power to touch my heart, to hold me back from the ruin into which I am about to plunge, to make me useful to my fellows—a man, and not a drunkard." Whispering these conclusions to myself, I am urged to brave public opinion, and make two lives happy. I say to myself, or rather my desires say to me—"What sin is there in this? Adultery? No; for a marriage without love is the coarsest of all adulteries. What tie binds a man and woman together—that formula of license pronounced by the priest, which the law has recognised as a 'legal bond'? Surely not this only, for marriage is but a partnership—a contract of mutual fidelity—and in all contracts the violation of the terms of agreement by one of the contracting persons absolves the other. Mrs. Frere is then absolved, by her husband's act. I cannot but think so. But is she willing to risk the shame of divorce or legal offence? Perhaps. Is she fitted by temperament to bear such a burden of contumely as must needs fall upon her? Will she not feel disgust at the man who entrapped her into shame? Do not the comforts which surround her compensate for the lack of affection?" And so the torturing catechism continues, until I am driven mad with doubt, love, and despair.

Of course I am wrong; of course I outrage my character as a priest; of course, I endanger—according to the creed I teach—my soul and hers. But priests, unluckily, have hearts and passions as well as other men. Thank God, as yet I have never expressed my madness in words. What a fate is mine! When I am in her presence I am in torment; when I am absent from her my imagination pictures her surrounded by a thousand graces that are not hers, but belong to all the women of my dreams—to Helen, to Juliet, to Rosalind. Fools that we are of our own senses! When I think of her I blush; when I hear her name my heart leaps, and I grow pale. Love! What is the love of two pure souls, scarce conscious of the Paradise into which they have fallen, to this maddening delirium? I can understand the poison of Circe's cup; it is the sweet-torment of a forbidden love like mine! Away gross materialism; in which I have so long schooled myself! I, who laughed at passion as the outcome of temperament and easy living—I, who thought in my intellect to sound all the depths and shoals of human feeling—I, who analysed my own soul—scoffed at my own yearnings for an immortality—am forced to deify the senseless power of my creed, and believe in God, that I may pray to Him. I know now why men reject the cold impersonality that reason tells us rules the world—it is because they love. To die, and be no more; to die and, rendered into dust, be blown about the earth; to die, and leave our love defenceless and forlorn, till the bright soul that smiled to ours in smothered in the earth that made it! No! To love is life eternal. God, I believe in Thee! Aid me! Pity me! Sinful wretch that I am, to have denied Thee! See me on my knees before Thee! Pity me, or let me die!

Treatment

• Background information: *For the Term of His Natural Life* is an outstanding novel of the early settlement of Australia. It depicts the horror and suffering of the penal colonies and the system under which many convicts vanished without a trace. In 1869, Marcus Clarke visited Tasmania and wrote his account of convict times. Much of his writing is based on actual records and dramatized into the story of its main protagonist, Rufus Dawes. It shares the timeless qualities of *Wuthering Heights, Great Expectations* or other works about the darkness of human behavior.

• This selection will need careful editing. Refer to Chapter I, "How to Use This Book."

• The scene is set with Rev. North writing these thoughts in his diary. This may be too passive a structure for an audition situation and you may wish to change it to suit your needs.

"The Diary of a Rent Striker"
New York Herald Tribune, 1964
Suggested age and gender: Broad age range; female
Recommended for: OB, DS

Summary

This piece is the diary of Innocencia Flores, mother of four, living in a decaying tenement in New York's East Harlem.

At the time this diary was written, she had just organized a rent strike with other tenants in her building.

Diary

WEDNESDAY, FEB. 5—I got up at 6:45. The first thing to do was light the oven. The boiler was broke so not getting the heat. All the tenants together bought the oil. We give $7.50 for each tenant. But the boiler old and many things we don't know about the pipes, so one of the men next door who used to be superintendent is trying to fix. I make the breakfast for the three children who go to school. I give them orange juice, oatmeal, scrambled eggs, and Ovaltine. They have lunch in school and sometimes they don't like the food and won't eat, so I say you have a good breakfast. Miss Christine Washington stick her head in at 7:30 and say she go to work. I used to live on ground floor, and she was all the time trying to get me move to third floor next door to her because this place vacant and the junkies use it, and she scared the junkies break the wall to get into her place and steal everything because she live alone and go to work. I'm glad I come up here to live because the rats so big downstairs. We all say, "The rats is big as cats." I had a baseball bat for the rats. It's lucky me and the children never got bit. The children go to school and I clean the house and empty the pan in the bathroom that catches the water dripping from pipe in the big hole in the ceiling. You have to carry umbrella to the bathroom sometimes. I go to the laundry place this afternoon and I wash again on Saturday because I change my kids' clothes every day because I don't want them dirty to attract the rats. . . .

THURSDAY, FEB. 6—I wake up at six o'clock and I went to the kitchen to heat a bottle for my baby. When I put the light on the kitchen I yelled so loud that I don't know if I disturbed the neighbors. There was a big rat coming out from the garbage pail. . . .

FRIDAY, FEB. 7—. . . .The baby woke up at five o'clock. I went to the kitchen but this time I didn't see the rat. After the girls left for school, I started washing the dishes and cleaning the kitchen. I am thinking about their school. . . . My girl take Spanish in junior high school, and I said to her, "Tell your teacher I'm going to be in school one day to teach him Spanish because I don't know where he learns to teach Spanish, but it ain't Spanish.". . .

I'm pretty good woman. I don't bother anyone. But I got my rights. I fight for them. I don't care about jail. Jail don't scare me. If have to go to jail, I go. I didn't steal. I didn't kill nobody. There's no record for me. But if I have to go, I go.

SATURDAY, FEB. 8—. . . .a tenant called me and asked me what was new in the building. She wanted to know about the junkies. . . .I'm not ascared of the junkies. I open the door and I see the junkies, I tell them to go or I call the police. Many people scared of them, but they scared of my face. I got baseball bat for the rats and for the junkies. . . .I know my rights and I know my self-respect. . . .

MONDAY, FEB. 10—. . . .At 9:30 a man came to fix the rat holes. He charged me only $3!. . .

TUESDAY, FEB. 11—. . . .We had no steam, the boiler is not running good. I feel miserable. . . .Living in a cold apartment is terrible. . . .

WEDNESDAY, FEB. 12—. . . .It still so cold the children trembling. You feel like crying looking your children in this way.

I think if I stay a little longer in this kind of living I'm going to be a dead duck. . . .My only weapon is my vote. This year I *don't vote* for nobody. . . .At least I clean my house and you could eat on the floor. The rest of the day I didn't do nothing. I was so mad all day long. I cooked a big pot of soup. . . .

FRIDAY, FEB. 14—. . . .I didn't write this about Friday in my book until this Saturday morning, because Friday night I sick and so cold. . . .

. . .It is really hard to believe that this happens in New York and richest city in the world. But such is Harlem and hope. Is this the way to live? I rather go to the Moon in the next trip.

Treatment

• See Treatment from *Even Cowgirls Get the Blues* and *Catcher in the Rye.* In addition:

• A typical week in the life of Innocencia Flores is characterized by frustration and unhappiness. Somehow she manages to cope. She survives a battle against junkies, rats, hostile landlords, and building inspectors by fighting back. "I see junkies, I tell them to go or I call the police. Many people scared of them, but they scared of my face. I got baseball bat for the rats and for the junkies. . .I know my rights and I know my self-respect."

• It is important to sense the *routine* of her life. Her circumstances never change but her reactions to them do. Some days she appears hopeful while other days she is discouraged and bitter.

• I have seen this selection work well as a scene—the other actor playing the role of interviewer.

Children in Jail by Thomas J. Cottle

Paperback edition: Beacon Press, 1977

Chapter 22: "I'm Crying 'Cause They Took Away My Future."

Begins: Page 35: "First thing I realized, man, I didn't know the time."

Ends: Page 38: "So I don't know."

Suggested age and gender: Broad age range; male

Recommended for: REP, OB, DS, A

Summary

Fernall Hoover had brains, charm, and good looks. Lacking the proper support system (an insensitive mother, absentee father) to help channel those attributes into a positive life style, he ended up going to prison at an early age. He was sentenced to five years for breaking and entering and carrying a gun.

In this piece he describes his prison experience.

As with the other selection from *Children in Jail*, the book provides detailed background material about Fernall Hoover's life.

Excerpt

. . .I'm crying in there, man, like I was this little boy or something. I'm really crying. I ain't shitting you. I'm crying 'cause I ain't got no future. I'm like my little brother used to get when we'd take away his toy or this blanket he carried around everywhere. Sitting on the floor crying so loud, you know, no one could shut him up. I'm crying 'cause they took away my future. I try to pull myself together, man. I say, "Okay, man, hold on, pull yourself together. Forget about this long future, this rest of your life stuff. You just be calm now, stop crying and start thinking about tomorrow." That's how I'm talking to myself. Just like that. So I try to settle down. "Forget the future," I say to myself. "Just tomorrow." Then, man, like it started raining or something, I'm crying all over again.

Treatment

See Treatment from *Even Cowgirls Get the Blues* (section on images) and *Catcher in the Rye* (final paragraph). In addition:

• All the selections are contemporary and deal with controversial issues of today.

• Language is descriptive and powerful.

• All of these men and women want desperately to be heard. Whether in the form of a confession or a remembrance, they struggle to express their thoughts and feelings.

• Life gave all of these characters an unfair shake at a very early age. We can assume they want to *mend* their situations—change their role(s) as life's protagonists. They search for peace of mind, forgiveness, freedom, and if they can get it—happiness.

• Make specific decisions regarding who you are talking to and what you need from that person.

Children in Jail by Thomas J. Cottle

Paperback edition: Beacon Press, 1977

Chapter 1: "That Kid Will End Up Killing Somebody"

Begins: Page 16: "I'd never been sick before."

Ends: Page 20: "I'm getting to think it really is only a matter of time."

Suggested age and gender: Broad age range; male or female

Recommended for: REP, OB, DS, A

Summary

Thomas Cottle's *Children in Jail* provides extensive background material on Bobbie Dijon. Her life of crime began at the age of thirteen, when she perpetrated such misdemeanors as fighting and shoplifting. It was only a matter of time before she was put behind bars to await trial for the murder of a neighbor. Here she recounts in remarkable detail her experiences in prison.

Excerpt

. . . That time I was vomiting? They said I was faking. . .They said that the vomit was real but I was sticking my finger down my throat to make myself vomit. You believe that? Can you see me having this conversation with a matron about whether or not I vomit 'cause I really have to or 'cause I'm sticking my finger down my throat so I can get a little attention? It's ridiculous. . .It's like that time in court when all these big shots were talking about the murder of that slob, Ben Colsey, and all I could think about was how stupid a name Arnold is. . . .I'm crying most of the time too, feeling sorry for myself like an old dog. But inside my head I'm saying, "Boy, this is terrific. I don't have to be in school anymore talking about mathematics or the Middle Ages. . .Now I get to talk to a matron, a real live woman who gets paid by the state, about vomiting.

Treatment

See Treatment from *Children in Jail* (Fernall Hoover).

Raging Bull by Jake La Motta with Joseph Carter and Peter Savage

Paperback edition: Bantam Books, Inc., 1980

Chapter 1

Begins: Page 1: "I was sixteen and a hard core, what they now call a juvenile delinquent."

Ends: Page 3: "Back then you knew that all you would ever get would be what you could steal."

Suggested age and gender: Broad age range; male

Recommended for: REP, OB, DS, A

Summary

The American public came to know Jake La Motta as a rapist, murderer, thief, and convict. He emerged from this sordid life to become a "hero of the slums" and finally the middleweight boxing champion of the world.

In this selection, he remembers his youth—memories of indigence and repression while growing up in a Bronx tenement.

Excerpt

Now, sometimes, at night, when I think back, I feel like I'm looking at an old black-and-white movie of myself. Why it should be black-and-white I don't know, but it is. Not a good movie, either, jerky, with gaps in it, a string of poorly lit sequences, some of them with no beginning and some with no end. No musical score, just sometimes the sound of a police siren or a pistol shot. And almost all of it happens at night, as if I lived my whole life at night.

. . .What I remember about the tenement as much as anything else is the smell. It's impossible to describe the smell of a tenement to someone who's never lived in one. You can't just put your head in the door and sniff. You have to live there, day and night, summer and winter, so the smell gets a chance to sink into your soul. There's all the dirt that the super never really manages to get clean even on the days when he does an hour's work, and this dirt has a smell, gray and dry and, after you've smelled it long enough, suffocating. And diapers. The slobs who live in tenements are always having kids, and naturally they don't have the money for any diaper service, so the old lady is always boiling diapers on the back of the stove and after a while the smell gets into the walls.

Treatment

See Treatment from *Children in Jail* (Fernall Hoover).

These two pieces are taken from the Memphis Police Department Sex Crime Squad's *1973 Rape Investigations Report.*

Suggested age and gender: Broad age range; female

Recommended for: REP, OB, DS

These two selections (see following page) are both testimonies from young rape victims. They appear in their entirety and can conceivably be edited into one piece.

I.

Okay, I was 14 years old at the time. School had let out, and I was walking home because I didn't have enough money for carfare. This guy saw me on the street or I saw him, and he said, "Hey, are you looking for a job?" Wow, I thought to myself, how did he know I was looking for a job? So I said, "Yeah, why?" And he said, "Because I know someone, a friend of mine, who's looking for someone to work part-time in his office." So I said, "Where's your friend's office?" and he said, "I'm not doin' anything, I'll walk you over there right now." I told him my mother was expecting me home. I said, "Why don't you just tell me where it is?" He said it would be better if he went with me because he had the connections. He said, "Why don't you call your mother and tell her you'll be home later?" We walked to a phone booth and this guy gave me a dime. He actually gave me a dime to call my mother. I called and said, "Ma, I got a job. I'm going over there right now."

He walked me over to this building and then he told me to wait downstairs and he'd go up and see if his friend was in. I thought that was a little odd, I didn't see why I had to wait downstairs, but I waited around and in a while he came back and said we could go upstairs. We went into this place and there was nothing in it but a dirty mattress. The guy locked the door real quick and then I knew what was happening. I started to cry. I was a virgin. I pleaded with him not to touch me, but he did. It hurt. He hurt me. I was crying a lot.

Afterward he gave me twenty cents to get home. He had the nerve to ask for my phone number so he could call me again. He wanted to ask my mother if he could date me. I gave him the wrong number and a phony name. All I could think of was that I had to go home and face my family, right? I had to go home, have dinner, smile and pretend nothing was wrong.

At dinner my ma kept asking, "What about your new job?" I said, "I don't want to talk about it, leave me alone. It didn't work out."

II.

I took a ride from a truck driver. I always thought truck drivers were good people to get rides from. My father used to drive trucks when he was young, and my cousin was a truck driver—they must be good people to take rides from, you know?

I got in the truck and he said to me, "Aren't you kind of young to be hitchhiking?" Right away I got scared. Then he told me that he'd have to pull off the highway and go to—I think it was Greenwich, or some other town. I thought, Oh God, he's going to pull off the highway and drive into the woods and rape me or stab me—because there had been a case I had just read about. I thought, My God, I have to jump out. I think he realized that this was on my mind because at that moment—we were on the highway—he started to attack me while he was driving. He started to beat me down and he started to rip off my blouse.

In the meantime the truck is swerving back and forth, I said—"Well, we're both going to die now." I remember at one point I was thinking, Why don't I just take the wheel and just swerve the fucking truck off the highway and end it? That was the only way I coud end it, but I didn't want to die. I don't know if this is what I imagine now, but I think there was some type of understanding between us that if I gave him all he wanted, he would let me go.

Treatment

See Treatment from *Children in Jail* (Fernall Hoover).

In Cold Blood by Truman Capote

Hardcover edition: Random House, Inc., 1965 (also available in
    paperback: NAL/Signet)

Final chapter: "The Corner"

Begins: Page 287: "There's nobody much I can talk to."

Ends: Page 287: "Dick was the best natured little kid."

Suggested age and gender: Middle-aged; female

Recommended for: REP, OB, DS, A

Summary

Mrs. Hickock is the mother of Richard Hickock, who sav-
agely murdered four members of the Clutter family in Holcomb,
Kansas on November 15, 1959. He was hanged for his crime on
a gallows in a warehouse in the Kansas State Penitentiary. Unable
to control her anguish during his trial, Mrs. Hickock had to be
led out of the courtroom by a woman reporter. In the scene she
reminisces about her own life and that of her son Richard's. "But
he was sweet, Dick was the best natured little kid."

Excerpt:

There's nobody much I can talk to. I don't mean people haven't
been kind, neighbors and all. . . .Everybody here has gone out
of their way to be friendly. The waitress over at the place where
we take our meals, she puts ice cream on the pie and don't
charge for it. I tell her don't, I can't eat it. Used to be I could
eat anything didn't eat me first. . . .It seems to me like people
are looking at me and thinking, well she must be to blame
somehow. The way I raised Dick. Maybe I did do something
wrong. Only I don't know what it could have been; I get head-
aches trying to remember.

Treatment

• There is a gentle, bittersweet quality about this speech and its speaker. Confused and tired, Mrs. Hickock traces the memories of her life in an attempt to understand what went wrong.

• Since this speech is so well written, many clues to the character are built into the text. Attack your work in the simplest, most obvious way.

• Note that this speech takes place in the ladies' room. This environment suggests Mrs. Hickock's need to escape the drama inside the courtroom, and be alone with her thoughts.

Sacco and Vanzetti

Taken from transcripts of the Public Record of the Trial of Sacco and Vanzetti in the courts of Massachusetts and subsequent proceedings, 1927–29

Suggested age and gender: Broad age range; male

Recommended for: REP, OB, DS

Summary

Sacco and Vanzetti were electrocuted on August 23, 1927 for the murder of two shoe factory employees. In these speeches, both men make a final plea of not guilty to spectators and members of the jury.

Both selections appear in their entirety and can conceivably be edited as one.

BARTOLEMEO VANZETTI

This is what I say: I would not wish to a dog or to a snake, to the most low and misfortune creature of the earth—I would not wish to any of them what I have had to suffer for things that I am not guilty of. I am suffering because I am a radical, and indeed I am a radical; I have suffered because I was an Italian, and indeed I am an Italian; I have suffered more for my family and for my beloved than for myself; but I am so convinced to be right that you could execute me two times, and if I could be reborn two other times I would live again to do what I have done already. I have finished; thank you.

NICOLA SACCO: I AM NEVER GUILTY

Yes sir, I am not an orator. It is not very familiar with me, the English language, and as I know, as my friend has told me, my comrade, Vanzetti will speak more long, so I thought to give him the chance.

I never know, never heard, even read in history anything so cruel as this court. After seven years prosecuting they still consider us guilty. And these gentle people here are arrayed with us in this court today.

I know the sentence will be between two classes, the oppressed class and the rich class, and there will be always collision between one and the other. We fraternize the people, tyrannize over them and kill them. We try the education of people always. You try to put a path between us and some other nationality that hates each other. That is why I am here today on this bench, for having been the oppressed class. Well. You are the oppressor.

You know it, Judge Thayer. You know all my life. You know why I have been here, and after seven years, we that you have been persecuting, me and my poor wife, and you still today sentence us to death. I would like to tell all my life, but what is the use? You know all about what I say before, and my friend—that is, my comrade—will be talking because he is more familiar with the language, and I will give him a chance.

My comrade, the kind man, the kind man to all the child, you sentence him two times, in the Bridgewater case and the Dedham case, connected with me, and you know he is innocent. You forget all this population that has been with us for seven years, to sympathize and give us all their energy and all their kindness. You do not care for them.

Among the peoples and the comrades and the working class there is a big legion of intellectual people which have been with us for seven years, not to commit the iniquitous sentence, but still the Court goes ahead. And I think I thank you all, you peoples, my comrades who have been with me for seven years, with the Sacco-Vanzetti case, and I will give my friend a chance.

I forgot one thing which my comrade remember me. As I said before, Judge Thayer know all my life, and he know that I am never guilty, never—not yesterday, nor today nor for ever.

Treatment

• The primary endeavor in this speech is to convince a judge and jury of your innocence. It may be helpful to recall a time in life when you felt very deeply about an issue and tried desperately to convince someone you were right. Crystallize that memory for yourself, then sprinkle it with energy, passion, and eloquence—qualities necessary to make this speech work.

• Since Sacco and Vanzetti were real people, you have the opportunity to research a role based on facts rather than assumptions. There is an abundance of background material available (including photographs) to assist you.

In particular:

Justice Crucified by Roberta Strauss Feuerlicht, New York: McGraw-Hill Book Co., 1977.

The Burning Bed by Faith McNulty

Hardcover edition: Harcourt Brace Jovanovich, 1980 (also available in paperback: Bantam Books)

Begins: Page 5: "Well, I don't know how it started or anything, but he began hitting me."

Ends: Page 7: "Just leave everything and never, never turn back."

Suggested age and gender: Broad age range; female

Recommended for: REP, OB, DS

Summary

Francine Hughes was an "ordinary" wife and mother from a small town in Michigan. By the age of twenty-nine, she had endured thirteen traumatic years of marriage to Mickey Hughes. He terrorized her with continual bouts of physical and mental violence. On March 9, 1977 she killed him.

This excerpt is from her testimony delivered during the trial later that year. Her speech taps a wide range of emotions: fear, sympathy, and outrage.

Excerpt

The kids were at the front door hollering they were hungry. And they were cold. I let the kids in. I just tried to stay quiet. Move quietly. Not say anything. Walking on eggs, because I didn't want him to start up again. I had the kids wash and we sat down to eat. None of us had eaten all day. I remember the salt on the food stinging my split lip where he'd hit me. The kids were trying to be quiet and I was trying to be quiet. Then Mickey came into the kitchen. He got a beer from the freezer and started yelling at me all over again. He pounded the table and the kids' milk spilled. It was dripping on the floor. The kids jumped up and started crying. Mickey made the kids go upstairs. Then he picked up the plates and dumped all the food on the floor. (*Witness is crying.*)

Treatment

See Treatment from *Sophie's Choice* (Sophie), "Diary of a Rent Striker," and *Even Cowgirls Get the Blues.*

In addition: You may wish to treat this piece as a scene rather than a monologue. Experiment with both possibilities.

Dispatches by Michael Herr

Paperback edition: Avon Books, 1978

Chapter I, Part II: "Breathing In"

Begins: Page 31: "One afternoon I mistook a bloody nose for a headwound."

Ends: Page 33: "I never went back to that outfit again either."

Suggested age and gender: Broad age range; male

Recommended for: REP, OB, DS

Summary

    Dispatches is a war correspondent's personal journal of the Vietnam War. In this piece he experiences how he would have behaved had he actually been wounded in combat.

Excerpt

When we fell down on the ground, the kid in front of me put his boot into my face. I didn't feel the boot, it got lost in the tremendous concussion I made hitting the ground, but I felt a sharp pain in a line over my eyes. . .Some hot stinking metal had been put into my mouth, I thought I tasted brains there sizzling on the end of my tongue, and the kid was fumbling for his canteen and looking really scared. . .and somewhere in there I got the feeling that it was him, somehow he'd just killed me.

Treatment

See Treatment from *Nam*.

Nam: The Vietnam War in the Words of the Men and Women Who Fought There by Mark Baker

Hardcover edition: William Morrow & Company, Inc., 1981

Begins: Page 91: "I didn't know shit about Vietnam or war."

Ends: Page 95: "That scared the shit out of me."

Suggested age and gender: Broad age range; male

Recommended for: REP, OB, DS, A

Summary

As the title suggests, *Nam* is the assembled memoirs of Vietnam veterans. What separates this selection from other pieces of its kind is the tender age of the character narrating. He was eighteen years old when he joined the Marines. We learn about the Vietnam experience through the eyes of a teenager. The "men" he describes were still chewing bubble gum and blowing bubbles while acting out a "cops and robbers" fantasy. . ."When I saw what was happening in Nam, I really wanted to cash in on it. Why not? It was like being invited to play with the big kids."

Excerpt

"You try to have fun with things. Ambush was fun. It's supposed to be professional, but it's not.

"Oh boy, here he comes. I got that one."

"This one is mine."

"Nah, I got this one. You got the last one."

"Man, this one's for me. Get your own."

"He's mine."

"Is not."

"Is too."

"Is not."

I loved flying helicopters because you went fast. It's power, like having a Corvette. I got to do something I'd wanted to do since I was a kid, which was touch clouds. When we went up high and there were clouds around, I'd dangle out the door and try to grab them, just to say I did it.

Treatment

• *Dispatches* and *Nam* are monologues which share a common theme: war. The very nature of this subject produces similar conditions and emotional levels in each character: anxiety, panic, fatigue. In addition:

• As with so many monologues in this book, it is important to create someone to talk to and decide what you need from that person. The text does not provide this information; therefore, you must invent it.

• See notes on "images" from *Even Cowgirls Get the Blues*. Keep in mind, not all actors need to substitute *other* images to recreate the reality of a speech. This is simply *one* way to work. Some actors are able to connect and respond to the images which are provided in the text, while others must go the substitution route.

• All of these scenes take place *outdoors*. The actor has to be aware of the physical aspects of this environment and incorporate that sensory information into the character.

• You can use material from several literary sources to build a show that centers on a common theme, such as war. The show can take the form of a compilation of scenes, a variety hour, or a one-man (-woman) show. Hopefully, this will tempt you to look further into material which expands on a given subject.

First Person America by Ann Banks
Paperback edition: Vintage Books, 1981
"Testifying": Lloyd Green
Begins: Page 250: "I'm in New York, but New York ain't in me."
Ends: Page 252: "I drinks to think."
Suggested age and gender: Middle-aged; male
Recommended for: REP, OB, DS

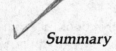

Summary

Lloyd Green is a Pullman porter from New York City. He is also a drunk. Just off from work, we find him at Eddie's Bar on St. Nicholas Avenue in Harlem, sharing his mixed feelings about New York City, then and now.

Excerpt

I'm in New York, but New York ain't in me. You understand? I'm in New York, but New york ain't in me. What do I mean? Listen. I'm from Jacksonville, Florida. Been in New York twenty-five years. I'm a New Yorker! But I'm in New York and New York ain't in me. Yuh understand? Naw, naw, you don't get me. What do they do? Take Lenox Avenue. Take Seventh Avenue. Take Sugar Hill! Pimps. Numbers. Cheating these poor people outa what they got. Shooting, cutting, backbiting, all them things. Yuh see? Yuh see what I mean? I'm in New York, but New York ain't in me! Don't laugh, don't laugh. I'm laughing but I don't mean it; it ain't funny.

Treatment

• Obviously Lloyd Green is intoxicated in this speech. There is a rule of thumb to follow when called on to play a drunk.

Drunkenness is simply a condition, another obstacle which you have to negotiate to get your point across. Once you establish drunkenness, forget about it and fight to be coherent. Your action is to *overcome* the drunkenness so you can communicate the words.

• An actor is so often asked to prepare two contrasting pieces for his/her audition. Lloyd Green could be very effective if performed along with a more conventional, upper-class character such as Henry Higgins.

Spoon River Anthology by Edgar Lee Masters (not reproduced
    in its entirety)
Macmillan Publishing Company, Inc.
"Plymouth Rock Joe"
Suggested age and gender: Broad age range; male
Recommended for: OB, DS

Summary

As with the next piece ("Elizabeth Childers") from *Spoon
River Anthology*, this selection is in the form of a confessional
monologue.

Plymouth Rock Joe has accused the men and women in
his town of having led lives of insignificance and pretense.

> Be chivalric, heroic, or aspiring,
> Metaphysical, religious, or rebellious,
> You shall never get out of the barnyard
> Except by way of over the fence
> Mixed with potato peelings and such into the trough!

Despite the angry, facetious quality of his speech, an underly-
ing layer of humor seems to emerge. He takes pleasure in saying
the things he does. After a lifetime of quietly observing these people, he is, at last, liberated.

Treatment

• The most suitable occasion for these two selections
(second selection on following page) from *Spoon River Anthology*, would be acting class. They force an actor to make
choices about a character where minimal background information is provided. Within the "confessional monologues" of Ply-

mouth Rock Joe and Elizabeth Childers lies the potential to create fully realized characters out of one's own imagination. Poems of this nature are excellent vehicles for learning the process of building a role.

• There are 244 characters to choose from in *Spoon River Anthology*. Here are a few other suggestions which my own students have successfully adapted to dramatic form: Zenas Witt, Russian Sonia, Lois Spears, Fiddler Jones, Dora Williams, and Yee Bow.

Spoon River Anthology by Edgar Lee Masters (not reproduced
   in its entirety)
Macmillan Publishing Company, Inc.
"Elizabeth Childers"
Suggested age and gender: Broad age range; female
Recommended for: DS, OB

Summary

The poetry of Edgar Lee Masters' characters describes the
spiritual and physical disintegration of a small American town
and its inhabitants. All are confessional monologues of tragic
existence.

In this piece, Elizabeth Childers laments the loss of her
child who died at birth. She comforts herself by realizing death
may very well be better than life.

> It is well, my child. For you never traveled
> The long, long way that begins with school days,
> When little fingers blur under the tears
> That fall on crooked letters.
> And the earliest wound, when a little mate
> Leaves you alone for another.

Treatment

See Treatment from *Spoon River Anthology* ("Plymouth
Rock Joe").

Growing Up Southern* edited by Chris Mayfield

Hardcover edition: Pantheon Books, 1981 (also available in paper-
    back: Pantheon Books)

Chapter 4: "Born for Hard Luck" by Allen Tullos Arthur "Peg
    Leg Sam" Jackson

This piece appears in its entirety.

Suggested age and gender: Broad age range; male

Recommended for: REP, OB, DS, A

Summary

In the author's own words:

Arthur 'Peg Leg Sam' Jackson took a fancy to playing the har-
monica and riding freight trains. One longtime friend remembers that Arthur, upon hearing an approaching train, once left
his mule harnessed in the field and ran for the railroad tracks.
He was gone for months.

   Peg's stories of hoboing, wandering, and odd jobbing re-
construct the plight of countless creative Southern men who
could find few satisfactory outlets in their lives.
Peg Leg Sam is a character equipped with a sense of humor
and the courage to persevere.

I rode more freight trains than days I got to live. All around
through Florida, Alabama, Georgia, Louisiana, Texas. What
got away with me one time was that Southern Pacific. I caught
it out of Louisiana one night—they called it the Sunset Limited. And it never did stop for nothing out through the sandy
desert. I was hungry, my God! Stomach thought my throat
was cut. When it got to Los Angeles, the first garbage can I
seen, I rushed to it, heels went over my head.

   *This article originally appeared in *Southern Exposure* Magazine, Volume
III, no. 4, winter, 1976.

I know every hobo jungle. From Alexandria, Virginia—with the ice cars. We'd drink rubbing alcohol there. Sometime we'd kill a pig or a cow. Four or five of us would carry him back and boy we had a ball that night. Hoboes telling lies and I was in there with 'em. Up there in Toledo, Ohio—the biggest hobo convention in the world. We had a sign hanging up, "When you eat, wash the pan and hang it up again. Another hobo, our friend, may come in."

Oh, I had a good living. Didn't have no home, always followed the season. I'd go down in Florida when it got cold, sleep outdoors. I slept outdoors half my life.

When I had two good feet I could catch the trains making forty miles an hour. When I lost my foot, I'd catch them making twenty-five miles an hour. I hoboed more after I got it cut off. Never caught the front car, always the back car so it would whup me up behind it.

I lost my leg in Raleigh. I was coming out of Richmond. I had gone uptown and bummed some of those ends they cut off meat. I got me some ends and come on back down near the tracks and laid down, I was right tired. My buddy shook me and said, "Train coming." That's all I remember. I caught it but I don't know how I fell off. I believe my head bumped under that bridge. You seen them things hanging down at bridges? That's to warn you before you get to it. I believe I caught it that way, half asleep when I caught it.

When I found myself, I was laying down on the rails. I thought, "My old leg done gone to sleep." And I got up, looked down, and my shoe was cut off my foot. Shoe split wide open. I said, "Mhnn, mhnn." Never felt bad till then. I fell back down on the railroad and yonder come the yard master. "Hoboing was you?" I says, "Sho was." "Let me see what I can do for you." He called the ambulance. About that time about a thousand people were up on the bridge looking down on me. They lifted me out of there and carried me to St. Agnes Hospital. They might be done changed the name now. That's been about forty-six years ago.

You look at me, you look at a man that was born for
   hard luck.
I was born on the thirteenth day, on Friday, bad luck day.
I was born the last month of the year.
I was born the last week in the month.
I was born the last day in the week.
I was born the last hour in the day.

I was born the last minute in the hour.
I was born the last second of the minute.

To show you that I am in hard luck,
If I go up the street walking fast, I run over something.
If I go up the street walking slow, something runs over me.
I'm in such hard luck, if I'm sitting down, I'm in everybody's way.
I'm in such hard luck, that if it's raining down soup at this very minute,
Everybody would be standing there with a spoon, why I'd have a fork.
I'm in such hard luck that if my daddy was to die,
They'd make a mistake and bury me.
I'm in such hard luck,
If I was to die they'd make me walk to the cemetery.
I was born for hard luck.

—Arthur "Peg Leg Sam" Jackson

Treatment

• Who are you addressing in this speech? Create someone to talk to and make a decision about what you need from them; otherwise the speech will seem vague and insignificant.

• Resist the urge to go the sympathetic route with this character. Emotional recollections of painful memories could lead you down the wrong path. I do not think Peg indulges himself in sorrow and self-pity. He describes his experiences (hoboing, losing a leg) in a very matter-of-fact way. Hoboing is his job and he accepts the hazards of his profession. He almost seems excited and proud of his escapades.

• Peg's memory is sharp. He recollects his experiences in great detail, double-checking the facts to get the story right.

• For further reading see the original articles from *Southern Exposure* Magazine, Volume III, no. 4, winter, 1976.

Hillbilly Women by Kathy Kahn

Paperback edition: Doubleday & Company, Inc., 1972

Part Three: "I'm Proud To Be A Hillbilly."

Begins: Page 112: "My mother worked in the cotton mill here, where they made the gauze wrapping for Kotex."

Ends: Page 120: "I want a man that's as big as I am. . . .When I find him, I don't care if he digs outhouse holes for a living, I'm going to live with him."

Suggested age and gender: Broad age range; female

Recommended for: REP, OB, DS

Summary

Donna Redmond grew up in a cotton mill town in Southern Appalachia. She spent years trying to make it there and, when it became impossible, migrated to Atlanta. She now works as a receptionist in an insurance agency. Though her life is not really a success story, she has managed to survive and support herself and her two children. She is bright, compassionate, and outspoken.

Excerpt

One girl VISTA told me recently that I don't know anything about life because I had never been to college, never been to New York City. Said I didn't know anything about what's really going on, like campus riots and all that crap. I may live in my own little world, but as far as knowing anything about life, that's a bunch of bull. Cause you just don't get pregnant, get married at fifteen, get divorced, work to support your kids and yourself without knowing a little bit about where it's really at. . . .

I really have this thing with these VISTA's, them coming in here with this idea that we're a bunch of poor ignorant hillbillies. I'm proud to be a hillbilly. And if you don't like the way I talk, then, damn it, go home! And don't make fun of my Southern accent, and if I want to eat grits for breakfast. . .dang straight, I think grits are the greatest thing that come along. . . .

They've all come from upper-middle-class families, all had Mama and Daddy handing them everything they ever wanted, ever needed. And as for their college educations, take your college education and shove it.

Treatment

I watched an actress perform these two selections (second piece follows) from *Hillbilly Women* and took a few notes:

1. The actress performed the entire speech sitting on a log in an empty room, rising *once* to lace her work boots and light a cigarette. This simple approach on a simple set worked very well.

2. Her choice and execution of a "mountain dialect" (a harsh, gutteral sound) was both appropriate and effective.

3. Both selections were well edited. (See Chapter 1, "How to Use This Book," for tips on editing a lengthy piece.)

4. Quite clearly, Shirley Sommerour and Donna Redmond are tough, courageous women. What impressed me about this particular performance was the actress's ability to uncover those qualities which are less apparent: sensitivity, femininity, and a sense of humor. You have to dig a little deeper to find these levels but your efforts will be worth the trouble. The reward is a lively, three-dimensional character.

Hillbilly Women by Kathy Kann

Paperback edition: Doubleday & Company, Inc., 1972

Part Three: "My Grandpa Always Taught Me to Fight."

Begins: Page 101: At one time Auraria was better known for gold then even California."

Ends: Page 109: "Later, I found out from a doctor that the little white pill was LSD."

Suggested age and gender: Broad age range; female

Recommended for: REP, OB, DS

Summary

Shirley Sommerour is a hard-working hillbilly woman from Southern Appalachia. Ostracized from family and community because of her illegitimacy, Shirley has had to fight a constant struggle for survival. Her pride, strength, and courage assist that struggle.

Excerpt

I went to work at Pine Tree Carpet Mills when I'd just hit my nineteenth birthday. . . .

One thing that happens in the mill is women are getting a lot of gas from the two machines where the men are operating machines run on butane gas. Women that sits behind these machines have almost passed out from the gas those machines throw off. That gas is bad. It burns us in our eyes and we have to breathe it in. . . .

There are pills being used by women in the mill. . . .The pills can be got by just snapping your fingers. You can get them through the black market here. One pill they use is the "green heart" and another is the "speckled bird.". . .

Once, when I was feeling real bad, a woman come to me with a little bitty white pill. Well, I wasn't too sure about the

pill so I only took half of it. . . .Then about three weeks later
I began having nightmares. I'd see the most terrible monsters
you'd ever imagined. Later, I found out from a doctor that the
little white pill was LSD.

Treatment

See Treatment from *Hillbilly Women:* "Donna Redmond."

"Weary with Toil" by William Shakespeare

1596

Suggested age and gender: Broad age range; male or female

Sonnet 27

Weary with toil, I haste me to my bed,
The dear repose for limbs with travel tired.
But then begins a journey in my head,
To work my mind, when body's work's expired.
For then my thoughts, from far where I abide,
Intend a zealous pilgrimage to thee,
And keep my drooping eyelids open wide,
Looking on darkness which the blind do see.
Save that my soul's imaginary sight
Presents thy shadow to my sightless view,
Which, like a jewel hung in ghastly night,
Makes black night beauteous and her old face new.
  Lo, thus by day my limbs, by night my mind,
  For thee and for myself no quiet find.

"That Time of Year" by William Shakespeare

1598

Suggested age and gender: Middle-aged; male or female

Sonnet 73

That time of year thou mayst in me behold
When yellow leaves, or none, or few, do hang
Upon those boughs which shake against the cold,
Bare ruined choirs where late the sweet birds sang.
In me thou see'st the twilight of such day
As after sunset fadeth in the west,
Which by and by black night doth take away,
Death's second self, that seals up all in rest.
In me thou see'st the glowing of such fire,
That on the ashes of his youth doth lie
As the deathbed whereon it must expire,
Consumed with that which it was nourished by.
   This thou perceivest, which makes thy love more strong,
   To love that well which thou must leave ere long.

"Let Me Not to the Marriage of True Minds" by William Shakespeare

1598

Suggested age and gender: Broad age range; male or female

Sonnet 116

Let me not to the marriage of true minds
Admit impediments. Love is not love
Which alters when it alteration finds,
Or bends with the remover to remove.
Oh no! It is an ever-fixed mark
That looks on tempests and is never shaken.
It is the star to every wandering bark,
Whose worth's unknown, although his height be taken.
Love's not Time's fool, though rosy lips and cheeks
Within his bending sickle's compass come.
Love alters not with his brief hours and weeks,
But bears it out even to the edge of doom.
   If this be error and upon me proved,
   I never writ, nor no man ever loved.

The Common Muse: An Anthology of Popular British Ballads and Poetry (XVth–XXth Centuries)

Edited by V. de Sola Pinto and A. E. Rodway

Philosophical Library, Inc., 1957

"My Thing is My Own"

Suggested age and gender: Broad age range; female

Note: If you audition for a classical theatre company and are asked to sing, this selection as well as the two which follow can easily be set to a simple tune. They are a wonderful departure from the usual Broadway fare and better suited to accompany your classical audition since they are similar in period and style.

I a tender young Maid have been courted by many,
Of all sorts and Trades as ever was any:
A spruce Haberdasher first spake me fair,
But I would have nothing to do with Small ware.
    My thing is my own, and I'll keep it so still,
    Yet other young Lasses may do what they will.

A sweet scented Courtier did give me a Kiss,
And promis'd me Mountains if I would be his,
But I'll not believe him, for it is too true,
Some Courtiers do promise much more than they do.
    My thing is my own, and I'll keep it so still,
    Yet other young Lasses may do what they will.

A fine Man of Law did come out of the Strand,
To plead his own Cause with his Fee in his Hand;
He made a brave Motion but that would not do,
For I did dismiss him, and Nonsuit him too.
    My thing is my own, and I'll keep it so still,
    Yet other young Lasses may do what they will.

Next came a young Fellow, a notable Spark,
(With Green Bag and Inkhorn, a Justice's Clark)
He pull'd out his Warrant to make all appear,
But I sent him away with a Flea in his Ear.

My thing is my own, and I'll keep it so still,
Yet other young Lasses may do what they will.

A Master of Musick came with an intent,
To give me a Lesson on my Instrument,
I thank'd him for nothing, but bid him be gone,
For my little Fiddle should not be plaid on.
My thing is my own, and I'll keep it so still,
Yet other young Lasses may do what they will.

An Usurer came with abundance of cash,
But I had no mind to come under his Lash,
He profer'd me Jewels, and great store of Gold,
But I would not Mortgage my little Free-hold.
My thing is my own, and I'll keep it so still,
Yet other young Lasses may do what they will.

A blunt Lieutenant surpriz'd my Placket,
And fiercely began to rifle and sack it,
I mustered my Spirits up and became bold,
And forc'd my Lieutenant to quit his stong hold.
My thing is my own, and I'll keep it so still,
Yet other young Lasses may do what they will.

A Crafty young Bumpkin that was very rich,
And us'd with his Bargains to go thro' stitch,
Did tender a Sum, but it would not avail,
That I should admit him my Tenant in tayl.
My thing is my own, and I'll keep it so still,
Yet other young Lasses may do what they will.

A fine dapper Taylor, with a Yard in his Hand,
Did profer his Service to be at Command,
He talk'd of a slit I had above Knee,
But I'll have no Taylors to stitch it for me.
My thing is my own, and I'll keep it so still,
Yet other young Lasses may do what they will.

A Gentleman that did talk much of his Grounds,
His Horses, his Setting-Dogs and his Grey-hounds,
Put in for a Course, and us'd all his Art,
But he mist of the Sport, for Puss would not start,
My thing is my own, and I'll keep it so still,
Yet other young Lasses may do what they will.

A pretty young Squire new come to the Town,
To empty his Pockets, and so to go down,
Did profer a kindness, but I would have none,
The same that he us'd to his Mother's Maid Joan.
  My thing is my own, and I'll keep it so still,
  Yet other young Lasses may do what they will.

Now here I could reckon a hundred and more,
Besides all the Gamesters recited before,
That made their addresses in hopes of a snap
But as young as I was I understood Trap.
  My thing is my own, and I'll keep it so still,
  Until I be marryed, say Men what they will.

The Common Muse: An Anthology of Popular British Ballads and Poetry (XV th–XXth Centuries)

Edited by V. de Sola Pinto and A. E. Rodway

Philosophical Library, Inc., 1957

"They're Shifting Father's Grave"

Suggested age and gender: Broad age range; male

They're shifting father's grave to build a sewer
They're shifting it regardless of expense
They're shifting his remains to make way for ten-inch drains
To suit some local high-class residents.

Now what's the use of having a religion
If when you die your bones can't rest in peace.
Because some high-born twit wants a pipeline for his s____t
They will not let poor father rest in peace.

But father in his life was ne'er a quitter
I don't suppose he'll be a quitter now.
He'll dress up in a sheet and he'll haunt that s____thouse
     seat
And never let those bastards s____t nohow.

Now won't there be an age of constipation
And won't those bastards howl, and rant, and rave
But they'll have got what they deserve, 'cause they had the
     bleeding nerve
To desecrate a British workman's grave.

The Common Muse: An Anthology of Popular British Ballads and Poetry (XVth–XXth Centuries)
Edited by V. de Sola Pinto and A. E. Rodway
Philosophical Library, Inc., 1957
"The Lass of Lynn's New Joy, for Finding a Father for Her Child"
Suggested age and gender: Broad age range; male or female

Come listen, and hear me tell
   the end of a Tale so true,
The Lass that made her Belly Swell,
   with *Marry and thank ye too.*

With many hard Sobs and Throws,
   and Sorrow enough (I wot)
She had wept Tears, the whole Town knows,
   could fill a whole Chamber-pot.

For Pleasure with Pain she pays,
   her Belly and Shame to hide
So hard all day she Lac'd her Stayers,
   as pinch'd both her Back and Side.

Oh! were not my Belly full,
   a Husband I'de have to Night;
There's *George* the *Tapster* at the *Bull*,
   I'm sure I'm his whole Delight.

This day on his Knees he Swore
   he Lov'd me about his Life,
Were not my Pipkin Crackt before,
   I vow I would be his Wife.

Her Mother that heard her, spoke,
   O take him at's word, said she,
A Husband, Child's, the only Cloak
   to cover a Great Belly.

Her Mother she show'd the way,
   and straight without more ado,
She took him to the Church next day,
   and *Marry'd and thank'd him too.*

111

But Oh! when he came to Bed,
    the saddest news now to tell ye;
On a soft place his hand he laid,
    and found she'd a Rising Belly.

At which he began to Roar,
    Your Fancy it has been Itching;
By th'Meat in your Pot, I find, you Whore,
    you've had a Cook in your Kitchin.

O fie, my dear Love, said she,
    what puts you into this Dump?
For what tho' Round my Belly be,
    it is only Fat and Plump.

Good Flesh it is all, ye Chit,
    besides, the plain truth to tell,
I've eat so much, the Sack-Posset
    has made my poor Belly Swell.

Nay, then I've wrong'd thee, he crys,
    I beg thy sweet pardon for't;
I'll get thee a Son before we rise,
    and so he fell to the Sport.

No, the Boy it was got before,
    the Midwife soon wisht him Joy;
But, Oh! e're full five Months were o're,
    she brought him a lusty Boy.

My Wife brought to Bed, says *George*,
    I hope she has but Miscarry'd;
A Boy! says he, how can that be,
    when we are but five Months Marry'd.

Five Months! has the man lost his Wits?
    crys Midwife, what does the Fool say?
Five months by Days, and five by Nights,
    sh'has gone her full time to a day.

The Child's all your own, by my truth,
    the pritty Eyes do but see,
Had it been spit out of your Mouth,
    more like you it could not be.

Nay then, my kind Gossips all,
    says George, let us Merry make;

I'll Tap a Barrel of stout Ale,
    and send for a Groaning-Cake.

The Gossips they Laugh'd and Smil'd,
    and Mirth it went round all through;
She'd found a Father for her Child,
    Hye, Marry and thank him too.

"Corinna's Going A-Maying" by Robert Herrick
1648

Suggested age and gender: Broad age range; male

Get up, get up for shame, the blooming morn
Upon her wings presents the gold unshorn.
  See how Aurora throws her fair
  Fresh-quilted colors through the air:
  Get up, sweet slug-a-bed, and see
  The dew bespangling herb and tree.
Each flower has wept and bowed toward the east
Above an hour since: yet you not dressed;
  Nay; not so much as out of bed?
  When all the birds have matins said
  And sung their thankful hymns, 'tis sin,
  Nay, profanation, to keep in,
Whenas a thousand virgins on this day
Spring, sooner than the lark, to fetch in May.

Rise, and put on your foliage, and be seen
To come forth, like the spring-time, fresh and green,
  And sweet as Flora. Take no care
  For jewels for your gown or hair:
  Fear not; the leaves will strew
  Gems in abundance upon you:
Besides, the childhood of the day has kept,
Against you come, some orient pearls unwept;
  Come and receive them while the light
  Hangs on the dew-locks of the night:
  And Titan on the eastern hill
  Retires himself, or else stands still
Till you come forth. Wash, dress, be brief in praying:
Few beads are best when once we go a-Maying.

Come, my Corinna, come; and, coming, mark
How each field turns a street, each street a park
  Made green and trimmed with trees; see how
  Devotion gives each house a bough
  Or branch; each porch, each door ere this
  An ark, a tabernacle is,

Made up of white-thorn, neatly interwove;
As if here were those cooler shades of love.
  Can such delights be in the street
  And open fields and we not see't?
  Come, we'll abroad; and let's obey
  The proclamation made for May:
And sin no more, as we have done, by staying;
But, my Corinna, come, let's go a-Maying.

There's not a budding boy or girl this day
But is got up, and gone to bring in May.
  A deal of youth, ere this, is come
  Back, and with white-thorn laden home.
  Some have despatched their cakes and cream
  Before that we have left to dream:
And some have wept, and wooed, and plighted troth,
And chose their priest, ere we can cast off sloth:
  Many a green-gown has been given;
  Many a kiss, both odd and even:
  Many a glance too has been sent
  From out the eye, love's firmament;
Many a jest told of the keys betraying
This night, and locks picked, yet we're not a-Maying.

Come, let us go while we are in our prime;
And take the harmless folly of the time.
  We shall grow old apace, and die
  Before we know our liberty.
  Our life is short, and our days run
  As fast away as does the sun;
And, as a vapor or a drop of rain,
Once lost, can ne'er be found again,
  So when or you or I are made
  A fable, song, or fleeting shade,
  All love, all liking, all delight
  Lies drowned with us in endless night.
Then while time serves, and we are but decaying,
Come, my Corinna, come, let's go a-Maying.

"The Solitary Reaper" by William Wordsworth
1807

Suggested age and gender: Broad age range; male

Behold her, single in the field,
　Yon solitary Highland Lass!
Reaping and singing by herself;
　Stop here, or gently pass!
Alone she cuts and binds the grain,
And sings a melancholy strain;
O listen! for the vale profound
Is overflowing with the sound.

No nightingale did ever chaunt
　More welcome notes to weary bands
Of travellers in some shady haunt,
　Among Arabian sands:
A voice so thrilling ne'er was heard
In spring-time from the cuckoo-bird,
Breaking the silence of the seas
Among the farthest Hebrides.

Will no one tell me what she sings?—
　Perhaps the plaintive numbers flow
For old, unhappy, far-off things,
　And battles long ago:
Or is it some more humble lay,
Familiar matter of to-day?
Some natural sorrow, loss, or pain,
That has been, and may be again?

Whate'er the theme, the maiden sang
　As if her song could have no ending;
I saw her singing at her work,
　And o'er the sickle bending;—
I listened, motionless and still;
And, as I mounted up the hill,
The music in my heart I bore,
Long after it was heard no more.

"Ode to the West Wind" by Percy Bysshe Shelley

1819

Suggested age and gender: Broad age range; male

O Wild West Wind, thou breath of Autumn's being,
Thou from whose unseen presence the leaves dead
Are driven like ghosts from an enchanter fleeing,

Yellow, and black, and pale, and hectic red,
Pestilence-stricken multitudes! O thou
Who chariotest to their dark wintry bed

The wingèd seeds, where they lie cold and low,
Each like a corpse within its grave, until
Thine azure sister of the Spring shall blow

Her clarion o'er the dreaming earth, and fill
(Driving sweet buds like flocks to feed in air)
With living hues and odours plain and hill;

Wild Spirit, which art moving everywhere;
Destroyer and preserver; hear, O hear!

II

Thou on whose stream, 'mid the steep sky's commotion,
Loose clouds like earth's decaying leaves are shed,
Shook from the tangled boughs of heaven and ocean,

Angels of rain and lightning! there are spread
On the blue surface of thine airy surge,
Like the bright hair uplifted from the head

Of some fierce Maenad, even from the dim verge
Of the horizon to the zenith's height,
The locks of the approaching storm. Thou dirge

Of the dying year, to which this closing night
Will be the dome of a vast sepulchre,
Vaulted with all thy congregated might

Of vapours, from whose solid atmosphere
Black rain, and fire, and hail will burst: O hear!

III

Thou who didst waken from his summer dreams
The blue Mediterranean, where he lay,
Lull'd by the coil of his crystalline streams,

Beside a pumice isle in Baiae's bay,
And saw in sleep old palaces and towers
Quivering within the wave's intenser day,

All overgrown with azure moss, and flowers
So sweet, the sense faints picturing them! Thou
For whose path the Atlantic's level powers

Cleave themselves into chasms, while far below
The sea-blooms and the oozy woods which wear
The sapless foliage of the ocean, know

Thy voice, and suddenly grow grey with fear,
And tremble and despoil themselves: O hear!

IV

If I were a dead leaf thou mightest bear;
If I were a swift cloud to fly with thee;
A wave to pant beneath thy power, and share

The impulse of thy strength, only less free
Than thou, O uncontrollable! If even
I were as in my boyhood, and could be

The comrade of thy wanderings over heaven,
As then, when to outstrip thy skiey speed
Scarce seem'd a vision—I would ne'er have striven

As thus with thee in prayer in my sore need.
O! Lift me as a wave, a leaf, a cloud!
I fall upon the thorns of life! I bleed!

A heavy weight of hours has chain'd and bow'd
One too like thee—tameless, and swift, and proud.

V

Make me thy lyre, even as the forest is:
What if my leaves are falling like its own?
The tumult of thy mighty harmonies

Will take from both a deep autumnal tone,
Sweet though in sadness. Be thou, Spirit fierce,
My Spirit! Be thou me, impetuous one!

Drive my dead thoughts over the universe,
Like wither'd leaves, to quicken a new birth;
And, by the incantation of this verse,

Scatter, as from an unextinguish'd hearth
Ashes and sparks, my words among mankind!
Be through my lips to unawaken'd earth

The trumpet of a prophecy! O Wind,
If Winter comes, can Spring be far behind?

"Ulysses" by Alfred, Lord Tennyson
1842

Suggested age and gender: Broad age range; male

It little profits that an idle king,
By this still hearth, among these barren crags,
Matched with an agèd wife, I mete and dole
Unequal laws unto a savage race,
That hoard, and sleep, and feed, and know not me.

I cannot rest from travel: I will drink
Life to the Lees: All times I have enjoyed
Greatly, have suffered greatly, both with those
That loved me, and alone; on shore, and when
Through scudding drifts the rainy Hyades
Vext the dim sea: I am become a name;
For always roaming with a hungry heart
Much have I seen and known,—cities of men
And manners, climates, councils, governments,
Myself not least, but honored of them all;
And drunk delight of battle with my peers,
Far on the ringing plains of windy Troy.
I am a part of all that I have met;
Yet all experience is an arch wherethrough
Gleams that untraveled world, whose margin fades
For ever and for ever when I move.
How dull it is to pause, to make an end,
To rust unburnished, not to shine in use!
As though to breathe were life! Life piled on life
Were all too little, and of one to me
Little remains; but every hour is saved
From that eternal silence, something more,
A bringer of new things; and vile it were
For some three suns to store and hoard myself,
And this grey spirit yearning in desire
To follow knowledge like a sinking star,
Beyond the utmost bound of human thought.

This is my son, mine own Telemachus,
To whom I leave the scepter and the isle—

Well-loved of me, discerning to fulfil
This labor, by slow prudence to make mild
A rugged people, and through soft degrees
Subdue them to the useful and the good.
Most blameless is he, centered in the sphere
Of common duties, decent not to fail
In offices of tenderness, and pay
Meet adoration to my household gods,
When I am gone. He works his work, I mine.

There lies the port; the vessel puffs her sail:
There gloom the dark, broad seas. My mariners,
Souls that have toiled, and wrought, and thought with
    me—
That ever with a frolic welcome took
The thunder and the sunshine, and opposed
Free hearts, free foreheads—you and I are old;
Old age hath yet his honor and his toil.
Death closes all; but something ere the end,
Some work of noble note, may yet be done,
Not unbecoming men that strove with Gods.
The lights begin to twinkle from the rocks;
The long day wanes; the slow moon climbs; the deep
Moans round with many voices. Come, my friends,
'Tis not too late to seek a newer world.
Push off, and sitting well in order smite
The sounding furrows; for my purpose holds
To sail beyond the sunset, and the baths
Of all the western stars, until I die.
It may be that the gulfs will wash us down;
It may be we shall touch the Happy Isles,
And see the great Achilles, whom we knew.
Though much is taken, much abides; and though
We are not now that strength which in old days
Moved earth and heaven, that which we are, we are:
One equal temper of heroic hearts,
Made weak by time and fate, but strong in will
To strive, to seek, to find, and not to yield.

"The Song of the Shirt" by Thomas Hood

1843

Suggested age and gender: Broad age range; female

With fingers weary and worn,
　　With eyelids heavy and red,
A woman sat, in unwomanly rags,
　　Plying her needle and thread—
Stitch! stitch! stitch!
　　In poverty, hunger, and dirt,
And still with a voice of dolorous pinch
　　She sang the 'Song of the Shirt.'

'Work! work! work!
　　While the cock is crowing aloof!
And work—work—work,
　　Till the stars shine through the roof!
It's Oh! to be a slave
　　Along with the barbarous Turk,
Where woman has never a soul to save,
　　If this is Christian work.

'Work—work—work,
　　Till the brain begins to swim;
Work—work—work,
　　Till the eyes are heavy and dim!
Seam, and gusset, and band,
　　Band, and gusset, and seam,
Till over the buttons I fall asleep,
　　And sew them on in a dream!

'Oh, Men, with Sisters dear!
　　Oh, Men, with Mothers and Wives!
It is not linen you're wearing out
　　But human creatures' lives!
Stitch—stitch—stitch,
　　In poverty, hunger, and dirt,
Sewing at once, with a double thread,
　　A Shroud as well as a Shirt.

'But why do I talk of Death?
    That Phantom of grisly bone,
I hardly fear its terrible shape,
    It seems so like my own—
It seems so like my own,
    Because of the fasts I keep;
Oh, God, that bread should be so dear,
    And flesh and blood so cheap!

'Work—work—work!
    My labour never flags;
And what are its wages? A bed of straw,
    A crust of bread—and rags.
That shattered roof—this naked floor—
    A table—a broken chair—
And a wall so blank, my shadow I thank
    For sometimes falling there!

'Work—work—work!
    From weary chime to chime,
Work—work—work,
    As prisoners work for crime!
Band, and gusset, and seam,
    Seam, and gusset, and band,
Till the heart is sick, and the brain benumbed,
    As well as the weary hand.

'Work—work—work!
    In the dull December light,
And work—work—work,
    When the weather is warm and bright—
While underneath the eaves
    The brooding swallows cling
As if to show me their sunny backs
    And twit me with the spring.

'Oh! but to breathe the breath
    Of the cowslip and primrose sweet—
With the sky above my head,
    And the grass beneath my feet;
For only one short hour
    To feel as I used to feel,
Before I knew the woes of want
    And the walk that costs a meal.

'Oh! but for one short hour!
    A respite however brief!
No blessèd leisure for Love or Hope,
    But only time for Grief!
A little weeping would ease my heart,
    But in their briny bed
My tears must stop, for every drop
    Hinders needle and thread!'

With fingers weary and worn,
    With eyelids heavy and red,
A woman sat, in unwomanly rags,
    Plying her needle and thread—
Stitch! stitch! stitch!
    In poverty, hunger, and dirt,
And still with a voice of dolorous pitch,—
Would that its tone could reach the Rich!—
    She sang this 'Song of the Shirt'!

"The Raven" by Edgar Allan Poe

1845

Suggested age and gender: Broad age range; male

Once upon a midnight dreary, while I pondered, weak and
weary,
Over many a quaint and curious volume of forgotten
lore—
While I nodded, nearly napping, suddenly there came a
tapping,
As of some one gently rapping, rapping at my chamber
door.
" 'Tis some visitor," I muttered, "tapping at my chamber
door—
Only this and nothing more."

Ah, distinctly I remember it was in the bleak December,
And each separate dying ember wrought its ghost upon
the floor.
Eagerly I wished the morrow;—vainly I had sought to
borrow
From my books surcease of sorrow—sorrow for the lost
Lenore—
For the rare and radiant maiden whom the angels name
Lenore—
Nameless here for evermore.

And the silken sad uncertain rustling of each purple
curtain
Thrilled me—filled me with fantastic terrors never felt
before;
So that now, to still the beating of my heart, I stood
repeating:
" 'Tis some visitor entreating entrance at my chamber
door—
Some late visitor entreating entrance at my chamber door;
This it is and nothing more."

Presently my soul grew stronger; hesitating then no longer,
"Sir," said I, "or Madam, truly your forgiveness I implore;
But the fact is I was napping, and so gently you came
  rapping,
And so faintly you came tapping, tapping at my chamber
  door,
That I scarce was sure I heard you"—here I opened wide
  the door;—
          Darkness there and nothing more.

Deep into that darkness peering, long I stood there
  wondering, fearing,
Doubting, dreaming dreams no mortals ever dared to
  dream before;
But the silence was unbroken, and the stillness gave no
  token,
And the only word there spoken was the whispered word,
  "Lenore!"
This I whispered, and an echo murmured back the word,
  "Lenore!"—
          Merely this and nothing more.

Back into the chamber turning, all my soul within me
  burning,
Soon again I heard a tapping something louder than before.
"Surely," said I, "surely that is something at my window
  lattice;
Let me see, then, what thereat is, and this mystery
  explore—
Let my heart be still a moment, and this mystery
  explore;—
          'Tis the wind and nothing more.

Open here I flung the shutter, when, with many a flirt and
  flutter,
In there stepped a stately Raven of the saintly days of
  yore.
Not the least obeisance made he; not a minute stopped or
  stayed he,
But, with mien of lord or lady, perched above my
  chamber door—
Perched upon a bust of Pallas just above my chamber
  door—
          Perched, and sat, and nothing more.

Then this ebony bird beguiling my sad fancy into smiling,
By the grave and stern decorum of the countenance it
     wore,
"Though thy crest be shorn and shaven, thou," I said, "art
     sure no craven,
Ghastly grim and ancient Raven wandering from the
     Nightly shore—
Tell me what thy lordly name is on the Night's Plutonian
     shore!"
               Quoth the Raven, "Nevermore."

Much I marvelled this ungainly fowl to hear discourse so
     plainly,
Though its answer little meaning—little relevancy bore;
For we cannot help agreeing that no living human being
Ever yet was blessed with seeing bird above his chamber
     door—
Bird or beast upon the sculptured bust above his chamber
     door,
               With such name as "Nevermore."

But the Raven, sitting lonely on that placid bust, spoke
     only
That one word, as if his soul in that one word he did
     outpour.
Nothing farther then he uttered; not a feather then he
     fluttered—
Till I scarcely more than muttered: "Other friends have
     flown before—
On the morrow *he* will leave me as my Hopes have flown
     before."
               Then the bird said, "Nevermore."

Startled at the stillness broken by reply so aptly spoken,
"Doubtless," said I, "what it utters is its only stock and
     store,
Caught from some unhappy master whom unmerciful
     Disaster
Followed fast and followed faster till his songs one burden
     bore—
Till the dirges of his Hope that melancholy burden bore
               Of "Never—nevermore."

But the Raven still beguiling all my sad soul into smiling,
Straight I wheeled a cushioned seat in front of bird and
     bust and door;

Then, upon the velvet sinking, I betook myself to linking
Fancy unto fancy, thinking what this ominous bird of
  yore—
What this grim, ungainly, ghastly, gaunt, and ominous
  bird of yore
              Meant in croaking "Nevermore."

This I sat engaged in guessing, but no syllable expressing
To the fowl whose fiery eyes now burned into my bosom's
  core;
This and more I sat divining, with my head at ease
  reclining
On the cushion's velvet lining that the lamp-light gloated
  o'er,
But whose velvet violet lining with the lamp-light gloating
  o'er
              She shall press, ah, nevermore!

Then, methought, the air grew denser, perfumed from an
  unseen censer
Swung by Seraphim whose foot-falls tinkled on the tufted
  floor.
"Wretch," I cried, "thy God hath lent thee—by these
  angels he hath sent thee
Respite—respite and nepenthe from thy memories of
  Lenore!
Quaff, oh quaff this kind nepenthe and forget this lost
  Lenore!"
              Quoth the Raven, "Nevermore."

"Phophet!" said I, "thing of evil!—prophet still, if bird or
  devil!—
Whether Tempter sent, or whether tempest tossed thee
  here ashore,
Desolate, yet all undaunted, on this desert land
  enchanted—
On this home by Horror haunted,—tell me truly, I
  implore—
Is there—*is* there balm in Gilead?—tell me—tell me, I
  implore!"
              Quoth the Raven, "Nevermore."

"Prophet!" said I, "thing of evil!—prophet still, if bird or
  devil!
By that heaven that bends above us—by that God we both
  adore—

Tell this soul with sorrow laden if, within the distant
Aidenn,
It shall clasp a sainted maiden whom the angels name
Lenore—
Clasp a rare and radiant maiden whom the angels name
Lenore."
        Quoth the Raven, "Nevermore."

"Be that word our sign of parting, bird or friend!" I
shrieked, upstarting—
"Get thee back into the tempest and the Night's Plutonian
shore!
Leave no black plume as a token of that lie thy soul hath
spoken!
Leave my loneliness unbroken!—quit the bust above my
door!
Take thy beak from out my heart, and take thy form
from off my door!"
        Quoth the Raven, "Nevermore."

And the Raven, never flitting, still is sitting, still is sitting
On the pallid bust of Pallas just above my chamber door;
And his eyes have all the seeming of a demon's that is
dreaming,
And the lamp-light o'er him streaming throws his shadow
on the floor;
And my soul from out that shadow that lies floating on
the floor
        Shall be lifted—nevermore!

Sonnets from the Portuguese by Elizabeth Barrett Browning
"I Lift My Heavy Heart Up Solemnly"
1846
Suggested age and gender: Broad age range; female

I lift my heavy heart up solemnly,
As once Electra her sepulchral urn,
And, looking in thine eyes, I overturn
The ashes at thy feet. Behold and see
What a great heap of grief lay hid in me,
And how the red wild sparkles dimly burn
Through the ashen greyness. If thy foot in scorn
Could tread them out to darkness utterly,
It might be well perhaps. But if instead
Thou wait beside me for the winds to blow
The grey dust up. . . .those laurels on thine head,
O my beloved, will not shield thee so,
That none of all the fires shall scorch and shred
The hair beneath. Stand further off then! go.

Sonnets from the Portuguese by Elizabeth Barrett Browning
"Belovèd, My Belovèd"
1846
Suggested age and gender: Broad age range; female

Belovèd, my Belovèd, when I think
That thou wast in the world a year ago,
What time I sat alone here in the snow
And saw no footprint, heard the silence sink
No moment at thy voice, but, link by link,
Went counting all my chains as if that so
They never could fall off at any blow
Struck by thy possible hand—why, thus I drink
Of life's great cup of wonder! Wonderful,
Never to feel thee thrill the day or night
With personal act or speech—nor ever cull
Some prescience of thee with the blossoms white
Thou sawest growing! Atheists are as dull,
Who cannot guess God's presence out of sight.

"I Felt a Funeral in My Brain" by Emily Dickinson
1861

Suggested age and gender: Broad age range; female

I felt a Funeral, in my Brain,
And Mourners to and fro
Kept treading—treading—till it seemed
That Sense was breaking through—

And when they all were seated,
A Service, like a Drum—
Kept beating—beating—till I thought
My Mind was going numb—

And then I heard them lift a Box
And creak across my Soul
With those same Boots of Lead, again,
Then Space—began to toll,

As all the Heavens were a Bell,
And Being, but an Ear,
And I, and Silence, some strange Race
Wrecked, solitary, here—

And then a Plank in Reason, broke,
And I dropped down, and down—
And hit a World, at every plunge,
And Finished knowing—then—

"I Like to See It Lap the Miles" by Emily Dickinson

1862

Suggested age and gender: Broad age range; female

I like to see it lap the miles,
And lick the valleys up,
And stop to feed itself at tanks;
And then, prodigious, step

Around a pile of mountains,
And, supercilious, peer
In shanties by the sides of roads;
And then a quarry pare

To fit its ribs,
And crawl between,
Complaining all the while
In horrid, hooting stanza;
Then chase itself down hill

And neigh like Boanerges;
Then, punctual as a star,
Stop—docile and omnipotent—
At its own stable door.

The Bab Ballads* by W. S. Gilbert
1869
"The Pantomime 'Super' to His Mask"
Suggested age and gender: Broad age range; male

Vast, empty shell!
Impertinent, preposterous abortion:
With vacant stare,
And ragged hair,
And every feature out of all proportion!
Embodiment of echoing inanity,
Excellent type of simpering insanity,
Unwieldy, clumsy nightmare of humanity,
I ring thy knell!

Tonight thou diest,
Beast that destroy'st my heaven-born identity!
Twelve weeks of nights
Before the lights,
Swamped in thine own preposterous nonentity,
I've been ill-treated, cursed, and thrashed diurnally,
Credited for the smile you wear externally—
I feel disposed to smash thy face, infernally,
As there thou liest!

I've been thy brain:
I've been the brain that lit thy dull concavity!
The human race
Invest *my* face
With thine expression of unchecked depravity:
Invested with a ghastly reciprocity,
I've been responsible for thy monstrosity,
I, for thy wanton, blundering ferocity—
But not again!

---

*The Bab Ballads were later to be part of the vast repertoire of operettas by Gilbert and Sullivan.

'Tis time to toll
Thy knell, and that of follies pantomimical:
A twelve weeks' run,
And thou hast done
All thou canst do to make thyself inimical.
Adieu, embodiment of all inanity!
Excellent type of simpering insanity!
Unwieldy, clumsy nightmare of humanity!
Freed is thy soul!

(*The Mask respondeth.*)

Oh! master mine,
Look thou within thee, ere again ill-using me.
Art thou aware
Of nothing there
Which might abuse thee, as thou art abusing me?
A brain that mourns *thine* unredeemed rascality?
A soul that weeps at *thy* threadbare morality?
Both grieving that *their* individuality
Is merged in thine?

The Bab Ballads by W. S. Gilbert

1869

"They'll None of 'Em Be Missed"

Suggested age and gender: Broad age range; male or female

As some day it may happen that a victim must be found,
 I've got a little list—I've got a little list
Of social offenders who might well be underground,
 And who never would be missed—who never would be
 missed!
There's the pestilential nuisances who write for
 autographs—
All people who have flabby hands and irritating laughs—
All children who are up in dates, and floor you with 'em
 flat—
All persons who in shaking hands, shake hands with you
 like *that*—
And all third persons who on spoiling *tête-à-têtes* insist—
 They'd none of 'em be missed—they'd none of 'em
 be missed!

There's the banjo serenader, and the others of his race,
 And the piano organist—I've got him on the list!
And the people who eat peppermint and puff it in your
 face,
They never would be missed—they never would be
 missed!

Then the idiot who praises, with enthusiastic tone,
All centuries but this, and every country but his own;
And the lady from the provinces, who dresses like a guy,
And who "doesn't think she waltzes, but would rather like
 to try";
And that *fin-de-siècle* anomaly, the scorching motorist—
 I don't think he'd be missed—I'm *sure* he'd not be
 missed!

And that *Nisi Prius* nuisance, who just now is rather rife,
 The Judicial humorist—I've got *him* on the list!
All funny fellows, comic men, and clowns of private life—

They'd none of 'em be missed—they'd none of 'em be missed!

And apologetic statesmen of the compromising kind,

Such as—What-d'ye-call-him—Thing'em-Bob, and like-wise—Never-mind,

And 'St—'st—'st—and What's-his-name, and also—You-know-who—

(The task of filling up the blanks I'd rather leave to *you*!)

But it really doesn't matter whom you put upon the list,

For they'd none of 'em be missed—they'd none of 'em be missed!

"Thirty Bob a Week" by John Davidson
1895

Suggested age and gender: Middle-aged; male

I couldn't touch a stop and turn a screw,
  And set the blooming world a-work for me,
Like such as cut their teeth—I hope, like you—
  On the handle of a skeleton gold key;
I cut mine on a leek, which I eat it every week:
  I'm a clerk at thirty bob as you can see.

But I don't allow it's luck and all a toss;
  There's no such thing as being starred and crossed;
It's just the power of some to be a boss,
  And the bally power of others to be bossed:
I face the music, sir; you bet I ain't a cur;
  Strike me lucky if I don't believe I'm lost!

For like a mole I journey in the dark,
  A-travelling along the underground
From my Pillar'd Halls and broad Suburban Park,
  To come the daily dull official round;
And home again at night with my pipe all alight,
  A-scheming how to count ten bob a pound.

And it's often very cold and very wet,
  And my missis stitches towels for a hunks;
And the Pillar'd Halls is half of it to let—
  Three rooms about the size of travelling trunks.
And we cough, my wife and I, to dislocate a sigh,
  When the noisy little kids are in their bunks.

But you never hear her do a growl or whine,
  For she's made of flint and roses, very odd;
And I've got to cut my meaning rather fine,
  Or I'd blubber, for I'm made of greens and sod:
So p'r'aps we are in Hell for all that I can tell,
  And lost and damn'd and served up hot to God.

I ain't blaspheming, Mr. Silver-tongue;
  I'm saying things a bit beyond your art:

Of all the rummy starts you ever sprung,
  Thirty bob a week's the rummiest start!
With your science and your books and your the'ries about
  spooks,
  Did you ever hear of looking in your heart?

I didn't mean your pocket, Mr., no:
  I mean that having children and a wife,
With thirty bob on which to come and go,
  Isn't dancing to the tabor and the fife:
When it doesn't make you drink, by Heaven! it makes you
  think,
  And notice curious items about life.

I step into my heart and there I meet
  A god-almighty devil singing small,
Who would like to shout and whistle in the street,
  And squelch the passers flat against the wall;
If the whole world was a cake he had the power to take,
  He would take it, ask for more, and eat it all.

And I meet a sort of simpleton beside,
  The kind that life is always giving beans;
With thirty bob a week to keep a bride
  He fell in love and married in his teens:
At thirty bob he stuck; but he knows it isn't luck:
  He knows the seas are deeper than tureens.

And the god-almighty devil and the fool
  That meet me in the High Street on the strike,
When I walk about my heart a-gathering wool,
  Are my good and evil angels if you like.
And both of them together in every kind of weather
  Ride me like a double-seated bike.

That's rough a bit and needs its meaning curled.
  But I have a high old hot un in my mind—
A most engrugious notion of the world,
  That leaves your lightning 'rithmetic behind
I give it at a glance when I say 'There ain't no chance,
  Nor nothing of the lucky-lottery kind.'

And it's this way that I make it out to be:
  No fathers, mothers, countries, climates—none;
Nor Adam was responsible for me,
  Nor society, nor systems, nary one:

A little sleeping seed, I woke—I did, indeed—
   A million years before the blooming sun.

I woke because I thought the time had come;
   Beyond my will there was no other cause;
And everywhere I found myself at home,
   Because I chose to be the thing I was;
And in whatever shape of mollusc or of ape
   I always went according to the laws.

I was the love that chose my mother out;
   I joined two lives and from the union burst;
My weakness and my strength without a doubt
   Are mine alone for ever from the first:
It's just the very same with a difference in the name
   As 'Thy will be done.' You say it if you durst!

They say it daily up and down the land
   As easy as you take a drink, it's true;
But the difficultest go to understand,
   And the difficultest job a man can do,
Is to come it brave and meek with thirty bob a week,
   And feel that that's the proper thing for you.

It's a naked child against a hungry wolf;
   It's playing bowls upon a splitting wreck;
It's walking on a string across a gulf
   With millstones fore-and-aft about your neck;
But the thing is daily done by many a one;
   And we fall, face forward, fighting, on the deck.

Through the Looking-Glass and What Alice Found There
by Lewis Carroll
1896
Chapter VIII: "The White Knight's Song"
Suggested age and gender: Broad age range; male

I'll tell thee everything I can;
    There's little to relate.
I saw an aged aged man,
    A-sitting on a gate.
"Who are you, aged man?" I said.
    "And how is it you live?"
And his answer trickled through my head
    Like water through a sieve.

He said "I look for butterflies
    That sleep among the wheat:
I make them into mutton-pies,
    And sell them in the street.
I sell them unto men," he said,
    "Who sail on stormy seas;
And that's the way I get my bread—
    A trifle, if you please."

But I was thinking of a plan
    To dye one's whiskers green,
And always use so large a fan
    That they could not be seen.
So, having no reply to give
    To what the old man said,
I cried "Come, tell me how you live!"
    And thumped him on the head.

His accents mild took up the tale:
    He said "I go my ways,
And when I find a mountain-rill,
    I set it in a blaze;
And thence they make a stuff they call
    Rowland's Macassar-Oil—

Yet twopence-halfpenny is all
    They give me for my toil."

But I was thinking of a way
    To feed oneself on batter,
And so go on from day to day
    Getting a little fatter.
I shook him well from side to side,
    Until his face was blue:
"Come, tell me how you live," I cried,
    "And what it is you do!"

He said "I hunt for haddocks' eyes
    Among the heather bright,
And work them into waistcoat-buttons
    In the silent night.
And these I do not sell for gold
    Or coin of silvery shine,
But for a copper halfpenny,
    And that will purchase nine.

"I sometimes dig for buttered rolls,
    Or set limed twigs for crabs;
I sometimes search the grassy knolls
    For wheels of Hansom-cabs.
And that's the way" (he gave a wink)
    "By which I get my wealth—
And very gladly will I drink
    Your Honour's noble health."

And now, if e'er by chance I put
    My fingers into glue,
Or madly squeeze a right-hand foot
    Into a left-hand shoe,
Or if I drop upon my toe
    A very heavy weight,
I weep, for it reminds me so
Of that old man I used to know—
Whose look was mild, whose speech was slow,
Whose hair was whiter than the snow,
Whose face was very like a crow,
With eyes, like cinders, all aglow,
Who seemed distracted with his woe,
Who rocked his body to and fro,

And muttered mumblingly and low,
As if his mouth were full of dough,
Who snorted like a buffalo—
That summer evening long ago
   A-sitting on a gate.

INDEX

NOW . . . Announcing these other fine books from Prentice-Hall—

THE MOVIE BUSINESS BOOK, by Jason E. Squire, ed. Until now, the inner workings of Hollywood have remained industry secrets. Here, the movie business is examined piece by piece in essays written personally by more than 40 film professionals—from directors and screenwriters to lawyers, distributors, and exhibitors. Renowned names in the field reveal their trade secrets, including Robert Evans, Mel Brooks, Sydney Pollack, Roberta Kent, Robert Laemmle, Jack Valenti, and more! A must for film students and avid movie fans.

$13.95 paperback, $24.95 hardcover

THE ACTOR'S SURVIVAL GUIDE FOR TODAY'S FILM INDUSTRY, by Renée Harmon. Shows aspiring actors how to get started in the film industry, including telelvision and commercial fields. Contains inside advice on finding the right photographer, writing a resume, finding an agent, interviewing, establishing public relations, and much more.

$6.95 paperback, $14.95 hardcover

To order these books, just complete the convenient order form below and mail to **Prentice-Hall, Inc., General Publishing Division, Attn. Addison Tredd, Englewood Cliffs, N.J. 07632**

Title	Author	Price*

Subtotal _____

Sales Tax (where applicable) _____

Postage & Handling (75¢/book) _____

Total $ _____

Please send me the books listed above. Enclosed is my check ☐ Money order ☐ or, charge my VISA ☐ MasterCard ☐ Account # _____

Credit card expiration date _____

Name _____

Address _____

City _____ State _____ Zip _____

Prices subject to change without notice. Please allow 4 weeks for delivery.

LIBRARY
ST. LOUIS COMMUNITY COLLEGE
AT FLORISSANT VALLEY.